A TREASURY OF PRAYER

A TREASURY OF PRAYER

THE BEST OF
E. M. BOUNDS
ON PRAYER IN A SINGLE VOLUME

COMPILED AND CONDENSED BY
LEONARD RAVENHILL

BETHANY HOUSE PUBLISHERS
Minneapolis, Minnesota 55438
A Division of Bethany Fellowship, Inc.

Seventeenth printing, 1990

A Treasury of Prayer
E. M. Bounds, Compiled by
Leonard Ravenhill

Library of Congress Catalog Card Number A–539865

ISBN 0–87123–543–9

Published by Bethany House Publishers
A Division of Bethany Fellowship, Inc.
6820 Auto Club Road, Minneapolis, Minnesota 55438

Printed in the United States of America

To
all those
who pray
"Lord, teach me to pray,"
this book
is
prayerfully dedicated

LEONARD RAVENHILL was born in 1907 in the city of Leeds, in Yorkshire, England. After his conversion to Christ, he was trained for the ministry at Cliff College. It soon became evident that evangelism was his forté and he engaged in it with both vigor and power. Eventually he became one of England's foremost outdoor evangelists. His meetings in the war years drew traffic-jamming crowds in Britain, and great numbers of his converts not only followed the Saviour into the Kingdom, but into the Christian ministry and the world's mission fields. In 1939, he married an Irish nurse, and from that union have come three sons. Paul and David are themselves ministers of the gospel, and Phillip is a teacher. Leonard and his wife now live near Lindale, Texas, from which place Ravenhill travels to widely scattered preaching points in conference ministry.

Other books by Ravenhill

Why Revival Tarries
Meat for Men
Sodom Had No Bible
Tried and Transfigured
America Is Too Young to Die

FOREWORD

by Dr. David Otis Fuller

The French Foreign Legion is world famous for its *esprit de corps* and daredevil spirit. It has a motto: "If I falter—push me on. If I stumble—pick me up. If I retreat—shoot me!" A far cry from the soft, silken ways of the average Christian of our day.

A sovereign God expects His own to intercede, to agonize for each other in this frightening age; these 1960's—Decade of Demons. Christians, multitudes of them, are faltering, stumbling, retreating before the triple threat of Red Communism, Roman Catholicism and Rotting Protestantism. But who prays? who cries to God? who cares? as civilization in convulsions comes to a rending crash, a climax, that no other age in history has ever reached? "Oh, let me alone, will you? I'm too busy making money . . . can't you *see* my plans are made for vacation, for fun? Why, the hottest TV show of the season is on Sunday and Wednesday nights! Don't talk to me about church or prayer meeting, *now!*"

PRAYER is our only hope. Our nation is doomed and damned unless born-again Christians, with their

backs to the wall, fall upon their knees beseeching a
holy God for mercy in this hour when America's
Ship of State, torpedoed by the enemy within, is poised
for the final plunge.

This "Treasury of Prayer" is worth its weight in
diamonds to the Christian who will make its every page
a heart matter. As the great Spurgeon said of Govett
and his writings one hundred years ago, so it may be
said of E. McKendree Bounds, "His pen produced the
purest gold." Very few preachers have access to the
writings of E. M. Bounds, but here you have a collection at once superb in diction and superabounding
in blessing.

It has been my privilege to know Leonard Ravenhill, the author of this splendid collection, for the past
several years. Never will I forget—nor will anyone
else who heard him—his series of dynamic, prayer-
filled messages given in our church for ten days, morning and evening. Several of our young people some
weeks later approached me, "When are we going to
have Rev. Ravenhill again?" They recognized his
power with God and with men. But it is no secret,
no insoluble mystery. He believes in the power of
prayer, and he practices what he believes.

NOW, Christian, is the hour for you and me to
prove God. But what in reality are we doing? *Tempting*
Him! To see how far we can go, how much we can
get away with, while souls drop into hell all around
us, and the cry of the Psalmist is heard in the land,
"I looked on my right hand, and beheld, but there was

no man that would know me; refuge failed me; no man cared for my soul" (Psalm 142:4).

I hold no brief for Voltaire the atheist, but his summary of history is all but perfect, "History is the sound of soft, silken slippers coming down the stairs and the thunder of hobnail boots going up." One can almost hear the thunder of the boots in America. Christian! in God's dear Name, hear me! You and I hold the key to revival in our individual lives. "If my people which are called by my name shall humble themselves and pray. . . ." Read this book, then join with me in confessing our utter failure and plead with our sovereign God, through His blessed Holy Spirit, "O Lord, revive thy work in the midst of the years, in the midst of the years make known; in wrath remember mercy" (Hab. 3:2).

David Otis Fuller
Wealthy Street Baptist Church
Wealthy Street
Grand Rapids, Michigan
U.S.A.

CONTENTS

ACKNOWLEDGMENTS

The publishers, the compiler, and the reading public wish to thank the Fleming H. Revell Company for their generous permission to reprint extensively from Dr. E. M. Bounds' books on prayer, which are copyrighted in their name.

A Treasury of Prayer is compiled from the following books by E. M. Bounds: *Power Through Prayer, Purpose in Prayer, The Necessity of Prayer, The Essentials of Prayer, The Weapon of Prayer, The Possibilities of Prayer*, and *The Reality of Prayer*.

The gleaning from the writings of Dr. E. M. Bounds for *A Treasury of Prayer* was made possible through the kindness of the Asbury Theological Seminary who made the books, now out of print, available to us. We are deeply grateful to Miss Susan Schultz, the seminary librarian, for her willingness and immediate cooperation in this matter. All profits through the publishing of this book will go towards the recruiting, training, and supporting of missionaries.

INTRODUCTION

by Leonard Ravenhill

In the Introduction of my book *Revival Praying*, I have acknowledged my long-time indebtedness to Dr. E. McKendree Bounds for his instructive and constructive writing on prayer. This present book is culled from the seven books that Dr. Bounds wrote on this great Bible theme of prayer.

Some of the initiated will note the omission of the title *Preacher and Prayer*. That book is in fact the same in text as *Power Through Prayer*. Much of its message is geared to the preachers, and that may account for the change of title. I believe that as long as books live, Dr. Bounds' books will live. He wrote with insight and foresight.

He anticipated the sickness of the Church of our day. He had prophetic foresight of the withering of the branch of prayer in the tree of the Church right now.

In my opinion, Bounds' writings on prayer have never been equalled. They are priceless, as my good friend Dr. David Otis Fuller has stated in the Foreword.

Dr. David Otis Fuller's Foreword is incisive and worthy of close reading. I am grateful to him for it.

Don't rest this book on a hard-to-reach shelf, nor on any shelf. (1) *Keep it handy.* (2) *Read it often.* (3) *Practice it always.* Then thou shalt have good success.

Prayerfully yours,
Leonard Ravenhill

WORD PORTRAIT OF DR. E. M. BOUNDS

by Homer W. Hodge

Rev. Edward McKendree Bounds was passionately devoted to his beloved Lord and Saviour Jesus Christ. His devotion was extraordinary in that he was praying and writing about Him all the time, except during the hours of sleeping.

God gave Bounds an enlargedness of heart and an insatiable desire to do service for Him. To this end he enjoyed what I am pleased to term a transcendent inspiration, else he could never have brought out of his treasury things new and old far exceeding anything we have known or read in the last half century.

Bounds is easily the Betelgeuse of the devotional sky. There is no man that has lived since the days of the Apostles that has surpassed him in the depths of his marvelous research into the Life of Prayer.

He was busily engaged in writing on his manuscripts when the Lord said unto him, "Well done, thou good and faithful servant, enter thou into the joys of thy Lord." His letters would often come to me in

Brooklyn, N.Y., in 1911, 1912 and 1913, saying, "Pray for me that God will give me new nerves and new visions to finish the manuscripts."

Wesley was of the sweetest and most forgiving disposition, but when aroused he was a man of the "keenest penetration with a gift of speech that bit like the stroke of a whip." Bounds was meek and humble, and never did we know him to retaliate upon any of his enemies. He cried over them and wept praying for them early and late.

Wesley was easily gulled. "My brother," said Charles on one occasion in disgusting accents, "was, I believe, born for the benefit of knaves." No man could impose on Bounds' credulity. He was a diagnostician of rare ability. Bounds shied away from all frauds in profession, and would waste no time upon them.

Wesley was preaching and riding all day. Bounds was praying and writing day and night.

Wesley would not allow any misrepresentation of his doctrinal positions in his late years. Bounds in this respect was very much like him.

Wesley came to his fame while yet alive. He was always in the public eye. Bounds, while editing a *Christian Advocate* for twelve years, was little known out of his church.

Wesley at eighty-six could still preach on the streets for thirty minutes. Bounds was able at seventy-five in the first hour of the fourth watch, to pray for three hours upon his knees.

Wesley, at the time of his death, had enjoyed fifty-six years of preferment. His name was on every tongue. Christianity was born again in England under his mighty preaching and organization. Bounds was comparatively unknown for fifty years but will recover the "lost and forgotten secret of the Church" in the next fifty years.

Wesley's piety and genius and popularity flowed from his early life like a majestic river. Bounds' has been dammed up, but now it is beginning to sweep with resistless force and ere long he will be the mighty Amazon of the devotional world.

Henry Crabbe Robinson said in his diary when he heard Wesley preach at Colchester, "He stood in a wide pulpit and on each side of him stood a minister, and the two held him up. His voice was feeble and he could hardly be heard, but his reverend countenance, especially his long white locks, formed a picture never to be forgotten." The writer of these lines gave up his pulpit in Brooklyn in 1912 to Rev. E. M. Bounds just ten months before his death. His voice was feeble and his periods were not rounded out. His sermon was only twenty minutes long, when he quietly came to the end and seemed exhausted.

Wesley had sufficient money and to spare during all his career. Bounds did not care for money. He did not depreciate it; he considered it the lowest order of power.

Wesley died with "an eye beaming and lips breaking into praise." "The best of all is God with us,"

Bounds wrote the writer of these lines. "When He is ready I am ready; I long to taste the joys of the heavenlies."

Wesley said, "The world is my parish." Bounds prayed as if the universe was his zone.

Wesley was the incarnation of unworldliness, the embodiment of magnanimity. Bounds was the incarnation of unearthliness, humility and self-denial. Wesley will live in the hearts of saints for everlasting ages. Bounds, eternally.

Wesley sleeps in City Road Chapel grounds, among his "bonny dead," under marble, with fitting tribute chiseled in prose, awaiting the Resurrection. Bounds sleeps in Washington, Georgia, cemetery, without marble covering, awaiting the Bridegroom's coming.

These two men held ideals high and clear beyond the reach of other men. Has this race of men entirely gone out of the world now that they are dead? Let us pray.

Homer W. Hodge

The Reality
Of Prayer

The potency of prayer hath subdued the strength of fire; it hath bridled the rage of lions, hushed anarchy to rest, extinguished wars, appeased the elements, expelled demons, burst the chains of death, expanded the gates of heaven, assuaged diseases, repelled frauds, rescued cities from destruction, stayed the sun in its course, and arrested the progress of the thunderbolt. Prayer is an all-efficient panoply, a treasure undiminished, a mine which is never exhausted, a sky unobscured by clouds, a heaven unruffled by storm. It is ·the root, the fountain, the mother of a thousand blessings.

—Chrysostom

CHAPTER ONE

THE REALITY OF PRAYER

Non-praying is lawlessness, discord, anarchy. Prayer, in the moral government of God, is as strong and far reaching as the law of gravitation in the material world, and it is as necessary as gravitation to hold things in their proper atmosphere and in life.

The space occupied by prayer in the Sermon on the Mount bespeaks its estimate by Christ and the importance it holds in His system. Many important principles are discussed in a verse or two. The sermon consists of one hundred and eleven verses, and eighteen are about prayer directly, and others indirectly.

Prayer was one of the cardinal principles of piety in every dispensation and to every child of God. It did not pertain to the business of Christ to originate duties, but to recover, to recaste, to spiritualise, and to re-inforce those duties which are cardinal and original.

With Moses the great features of prayer are prominent. He never beats the air nor fights a sham battle. The most serious and strenuous business of his

serious and strenuous life was prayer. He is as much
at it with the earnestness of his soul.

Intimate as he was with God, his intimacy did not
abate the necessity of prayer. This intimacy only
brought clearer insight into the nature and necessity
of prayer, and led him to see the greater obligations
to pray, and to discover the larger results of praying.
In reviewing one of the crises through which Israel
passed, when the very existence of the nation was in
peril, he writes: "I fell down before the Lord forty
days and forty nights." Wonderful praying and wonderful results! Moses knew how to do wonderful praying, and God knew how to give wonderful results.

*The whole force of Bible statement is to increase
our faith in the doctrine that prayer affects God, secures favors from God, which can be secured in no
other way, and which will not be bestowed by God
if we do not pray.* The whole canon of Bible teaching
is to illustrate the great truth that God hears and answers prayer. One of the great purposes of God in His
Book is to impress upon us indelibly the great importance, the priceless value, and the absolute necessity
of asking God for the things we need for time and
eternity. He urges us by every consideration, and
presses and warns us by every interest. He points us
to His own Son, turned over to us for our good, as
His pledge that prayer will be answered, teaching us
that God is our Father, able to do all things for us
and to give all things to us, much more than earthly
parents are able or willing to do for their children.

Let us thoroughly understand ourselves and understand, also, this great business of prayer. Our one great business is prayer, and we will never do it well unless we fasten to it by all binding force. We will never do it well without arranging the best conditions of doing it well. Satan has suffered so much by good praying that all his wily, shrewd and ensnaring devices will be used to cripple its performances.

We must, by all the fastenings we can find, cable ourselves to prayer. To be loose in time and place is to open the door to Satan. To be exact, prompt, unswerving, and careful in even the little things, is to buttress ourselves against the evil one.

Prayer, by God's very oath, is put in the very stones of God's foundations, as eternal as its companion, "And men shall pray for him continually." This is the eternal condition which advances His cause, and makes it powerfully aggressive. Men are to always pray for it. Its strength, beauty and aggression lie in their prayers. Its power lies simply in its power to pray. No power is found elsewhere but in its ability to pray, "For my house shall be called the house of prayer for all people." It is based on prayer, and carried on by the same means.

Prayer is a privilege, a sacred, princely privilege. Prayer is a duty, an obligation most binding, and most imperative, which should hold us to it. But prayer is more than a privilege, more than a duty. It is a means, an instrument, a condition. Not to pray is to lose much more than to fail in the exercise and enjoyment of a high or sweet privilege. Not to pray is to fail among lines far more important than even the violation of an obligation.

Prayer is the appointed condition of getting God's aid. This aid is as manifold and illimitable as God's ability, and as varied and exhaustless is this aid as man's need. Prayer is the avenue through which God supplies man's wants.

Prayer is the channel through which all good flows from God to man, and all good from men to men. God is the Christian's Father. Asking and giving are in that relation.

Man is the one more immediately concerned in this great work of praying. It ennobles man's reason to employ it in prayer. The office and work of prayer is the divinest engagement of man's reason. Prayer makes man's reason to shine. Intelligence of the highest order approves prayer. He is the wisest man who prays the most and the best. Prayer is the school of wisdom as well as of piety.

Prayer is not a picture to handle, to admire, to look at. It is not beauty, coloring, shape, attitude, imagination, or genius. These things do not pertain to its character or conduct. It is not poetry or music; its inspiration and melody come from heaven. Prayer belongs to the Spirit, and at times it possesses the spirit and stirs the spirit with high and holy purposes and resolves.

The possibilities and necessity of prayer are graven in the eternal foundations of the Gospel. The relation that is established between the Father and the Son and the decreed covenant between the two, has prayer as the base of its existence, and the conditions of the advance and success of the gospel. Prayer is the condition by which all foes are to be overcome and all the inheritance is to be possessed.

These are axiomatic truths, though they may be very homely ones. But these are the times when Bible axioms need to be stressed, pressed, iterated and reiterated. The very air is rife with influences, practices and theories which sap foundations, and the most veritable truths and the most self-evident axioms go down by insidious and invisible attacks.

More than this: the tendency of these times is to an ostentatious parade of *doing*, which enfeebles the life and dissipates the spirit of praying. There may be kneeling, and there may be standing in prayerful attitude. There may be much bowing of the head, and yet there may be no serious, real praying.

Prayer is real work.
Praying is vital work.
Prayer has in its keeping the very heart of worship.

Who can approach into God's presence in prayer? Who can come before the great God, Maker of all worlds, the God and Father of our Lord Jesus Christ, who holds in His hand all good, and who is all-powerful and able to do all things? Man's approach to this great God—what lowliness, what truth, what cleanness of hands, and purity of heart is needed and demanded!

Definition of prayer scarcely belongs to Bible range at any point.

Everywhere we are impressed that *it is more important and urgent that men pray, than that they be skilled in the homiletic didactics of prayer.*

This is a thing of the heart, not of the schools. It is more of feeling than of words.

Praying is the best school in which to learn to pray, prayer the best dictionary to define the art and nature of praying.

We repeat and reiterate. Prayer is not a mere habit, riveted by custom and memory, something which must be gone through with, its value depending upon the decency and perfection of the performance. Prayer is not a duty which must be performed, to ease obligation and to quiet conscience.

Prayer is not mere privilege, a sacred indulgence to be taken advantage of, at leisure, at pleasure, at will, and no serious loss attending its omission.

Prayer is a solemn service due to God, an adoration, a worship, an approach to God for some request, the presenting of some desire, the expression of some need to Him, who supplies all need, and who satisfies all desires; who, as a father, finds His greatest pleasure in relieving the wants and granting the desires of His children.

Prayer is the child's request, not to the winds, nor to the world, but to the Father.

Prayer is the outstretched arms of the child for the Father's help.

Prayer is the child's cry calling to the Father's ear, the Father's heart, and to the Father's ability, which the Father is to hear, the Father is to feel, and which the Father is to relieve.

Prayer is the seeking of God's great and greatest good, which will not come if we do not pray.

Prayer is an ardent and believing cry to God for some specific thing. God's rule is to answer prayer by giving the specific thing asked for. With it may come much of other gifts and graces.

Strength, serenity, sweetness, and faith may come as the bearers of the gifts. But even they come because God hears and answers prayer.

Revelation does not deal in philosophical subtleties, nor verbal niceties and hair-splitting distinctions. It unfolds relationships, declares principles, and enforces duties. The heart must define; the experience must realize.

Paul came on the stage too late to define prayer. That which had been so well done by patriarchs and prophets needed no return to dictionaries. Christ is himself the illustration and definition of prayer. He prayed as man had never prayed.

He put prayer on a higher basis, with grander results and simpler being than it had ever known.

He taught Paul how to pray by the revelation of himself, which is the first call to prayer, and the first lesson in praying.

Prayer, like love, is too ethereal and too heavenly to be held in the gross rams of chilly definitions. It belongs to heaven, and to the heart, and not to words and ideas only.

Prayer is no petty invention of man, a fancied relief for fancied ills.

Prayer is no dreary performance, dead and death-dealing, but is God's enabling act for man, living and life-giving, joy and joy-giving.

Prayer is the contact of a living soul with God. In prayer God stoops to kiss man, to bless man, and to aid man in everything that God can devise or man can need.

Prayer fills man's emptiness with God's fullness. Prayer fills man's poverty with God's riches. Prayer puts away man's weakness with the coming of God's strength.

It banishes man's littleness with God's greatness. Prayer is God's plan to supply man's great and continuous need with God's great and continuous abundance.

What is this prayer to which men are called? It is not a mere form, a child's play. It is serious, difficult work, the manliest, the mightiest work, the divinest work which man can do.

Prayer lifts men out of the earthliness and links them with the heavenlies. Men are never nearer heaven, nearer God, never more God-like, never in deeper sympathy and truer partnership with Jesus Christ, than when praying. Love, philanthropy, holy affiances, all of them helpful and tender for men—are born and perfected by prayer.

Prayer is not merely a question of duty, but of salvation. Are men saved who are not men of prayer? Is not the gift, the inclination, the habit of prayer, one of the elements or characteristics of salvation? Can it be possible to be in affinity with Jesus Christ and not be prayerful? *Is it possible to have the Holy Spirit and not have the spirit of prayer?* Is it possible to have the new birth and not be born to prayer? Is not the life of the Spirit and the life of prayer co-ordinate and consistent? Can brotherly love be in the heart which is unschooled in prayer?

We have two kinds of prayer named in the New Testament—prayer and supplication.

Prayer denotes prayer in general. Supplication is a more intense and more special form of prayer. These two, supplication and prayer, ought to be combined. Then we would have devotion in its widest and sweetest form, and supplication with its most earnest and personal sense of need. "Prayer gives us eyes to see God. Prayer is seeing God." The prayer life is knowledge without and within. All vigilance without, all vigilance within. There can be no intelligent prayer without knowledge within. Our inner condition and our inner needs must be felt and known.

It takes prayer to minister. It takes life, the highest form of life, to minister. Prayer is the highest intelligence, the profoundest wisdom, the most vital the most joyous, the most efficacious, the most powerful of all vocations. It is life, radiant, transporting, eternal life. Away with dry forms, with dead, cold habits of prayer! Away with sterile routine, with senseless performances and petty playthings in prayer!

Let us get at the serious work, the chief business of men, that of prayer. Let us work at it skillfully.

Let us seek to be adept in this great work of praying. Let us be master-workmen in this high art of praying. Let us be so in the habit of prayer, so devoted to prayer, so filled with its rich spices, so ardent by its holy flame, that all heaven and earth will be perfumed by its aroma, and nations yet in the womb will be blessed by our prayers. Heaven will be fuller and brighter in glorious inhabitants, earth will be better prepared for its bridal day, and hell robbed of many of its victims, because we have lived to pray.

Poverty of spirit enters into true praying. "Blessed are the poor in spirit, for theirs is the kingdom of heaven." "The poor" means paupers, beggars, those who live on the bounty of others, who live by begging. Christ's people live by asking. "Prayer is the Christian's vital breath." It is his affluent inheritance, his daily annuity.

In His own example, Christ illustrates the nature and necessity of prayer. Everywhere He declares that he who is on God's mission in this world will pray. He is an illustrious example of the principle that the more devoted the man is to God, the more prayerful will he be. The more divine the man, the more of the Spirit of the Father and of the Son he has, and the more prayerful will he be. And conversely, it is true that the more prayerful he is, the more of the Spirit of the Father and of the Son will he receive.

In the great events and crowning periods of the life of Jesus we find Him in prayer—at the beginning of His ministry, at the fords of the Jordan, when the Holy Spirit descended upon Him; just prior to the transfiguration, and in the Garden of Gethsemane. Well do the words of Peter come in here: "Leaving us an example that ye should follow in his steps."

There is an important principle of prayer found in some of the miracles of Christ. It is the progressive nature of the answer to prayer. Not at once does God always give the full answer to prayer but rather progressively, step by step. Mark 8:22 describes a case which illustrates this important truth, too often overlooked.

What are the limitations of prayer? How far do its benefits and possibilities reach? What part of God's dealings with man, and with man's world, is unaffected by prayer? Do the possibilities of prayer cover all temporal and spiritual good? The answers to these questions are of transcendental importance. The answer will gauge the effort and results of our praying. The answer will greatly enhance the value of prayer, or will greatly depress prayer. The answers to these important questions are fully covered by

Paul's words on prayer: "Be careful for nothing, but in everything by prayer and supplication, with thanksgiving, let your requests be made known unto God" (Phil. 4:6).

"Christ is all. We are complete in Him. He is the answer to every need, the perfect Saviour. He needs no decoration to heighten His beauty, no prop to increase His stability, no girding to perfect His strength. Who can gild refined gold, whiten the snow, perfume the rose, or heighten the colors of the summer sunset? Who will prop the mountains or help the great deep? It is not Christ and philosophy, nor Christ and money, nor civilization, nor diplomacy, nor science, nor organization. It is Christ alone. He trod the wine press alone. His own arm brought salvation. He is enough. He is the comfort, the strength, the wisdom, the righteousness, the sanctification of all men." —C. L. Chilton

Prayer is God's business to which men can attend. Prayer is God's necessary business, which men only can do, and that men must do.

Men who belong to God are obliged to pray. They are not obliged to grow rich, nor to make money. They are not obliged to have large success in business. These are incidental, occasional, merely nominal, as far as integrity to heaven and loyalty to God are concerned. Material successes are immaterial to God. Men are neither better nor worse with those things or without them. They are not sources of reputation nor elements of character in the heavenly estimates.

God is vitally concerned that men should pray.

Men are bettered by prayer, and the world is bettered by praying. God does His best work for the world through prayer.

God's greatest glory and man's highest good are secured by prayer. Prayer forms the godliest men and makes the godliest world.

God's promises lie like giant corpses without life, only for decay and dust, unless men appropriate and vivify these promises by earnest and prevailing prayer.

Promises are like the unsown seed, the germ of life in it, but the soil and culture of prayer are necessary to germinate and culture the seed.

Prayer is God's life-giving breath.

God's purposes move along the pathway made by prayer to their glorious designs. God's purposes are always moving to their high and benignant ends, but the movement is along the way marked by unceasing prayer. The breath of prayer in man is from God.

God has everything to do with prayer, as well as everything to do with the one who prays. To him who prays, and as he prays, the hour is sacred because it is God's hour. The occasion is sacred because it is the occasion of the soul's approach to God, and of dealing with God.

No hour is more hallowed because it is the occasion of the soul's mightiest approach to God, and of the fullest revelation from God.

Men are God-like and men are blessed, just as the hour of prayer has the most of God in it.

Prayer makes and measures the approach of God.

He knows not God who knows not how to pray.

He has never seen God whose eye has not been couched for God in the closet.

God's vision place is the closet. His dwelling place is in secret. "He that dwelleth in the secret place of the most High shall abide under the shadow of the Almighty."

He has never studied God who has not had his intellect broadened, strengthened, clarified and uplifted by prayer. Almighty God commands prayer; God waits on prayer to order His ways.

To God, prayer is what the incense was to the Jewish Temple. It impregnates everything, perfumes everything, and sweetens everything.

The possibilities of prayer cover the whole purposes of God through Christ.

God encourages us to pray, not only by the certainty of the answer, but by the munificence of the promise and the bounty of the giver. How princely the promise, "All things whatsoever..."! And when we super-add to that "whatsoever" the promise which covers all things and everything, without qualification,

exception or limitation, "anything," this is to expand
and make minute and specific the promise.

The challenge of God to us is, "Call unto me, and I
will answer thee, and show thee great and mighty
things which thou knowest not."

God gave us all things in prayer by promise because
He had given us all things in His Son. Amazing gift—
His Son!

Prayer is as illimitable as His own blessed Son.
There is nothing on earth nor in heaven, for time
or eternity, that God's Son did not secure for us.
By prayer God gives us the vast and matchless inheritance which is ours by virtue of His Son. God
charges us to "come boldly to the throne of grace."
God is glorified and Christ is honored by large asking.

That which is true of the promises of God is
equally true of the purposes of God. We might say
that God does nothing without prayer. His most gracious
purposes are conditioned on prayer. His marvelous
promises in the thirty-sixth chapter of Ezekiel are
subject to this qualification and condition: "Thus
saith the Lord God: I will yet for this be inquired
of by the house of Israel to do it for them."

Prayer affects God more powerfully than His own
purposes. God's will, words, and purposes are all subject
to review when the mighty potences of prayer come
in. How mighty prayer is with God may be seen as
He readily sets aside His own fixed and declared purposes in answer to prayer. The whole plan of salvation

had been blocked had Jesus Christ prayed for the twelve legions of angels to carry dismay and ruin to His enemies.

The fasting and prayers of the Ninevites changed God's purposes to destroy that wicked city after Jonah had gone there and cried unto the people, "Yet forty days and Nineveh shall be destroyed."

Almighty God is concerned in our praying. He wills it, He commands it, He inspires it. Jesus Christ in heaven is ever praying. Prayer is His law and His life.

The Holy Spirit teaches us how to pray. He prays for us "with groanings which cannot be uttered."

All these show the deep concern of God in prayer. It discloses very clearly how vital it is to His work in this world, and how far-reaching are its possibilities. Prayer forms the very center of the heart and will of God concerning men. "Rejoice evermore, pray without ceasing, and in everything give thanks. For this is the will of God in Christ Jesus concerning you."

Prayer is the pole star around which rejoicing and thanksgiving revolve.

Prayer is the heart sending its full and happy pulsations up to God through the glad currents of joy and thanksgiving.

By prayer God's name is hallowed. By prayer God's Kingdom comes. By prayer is His Kingdom established in power and made to move with conquering force swifter than the light. By prayer God's will is done till earth rivals heaven in harmony and beauty.

By prayer daily toil is sanctified and enriched, and pardon is secured, and Satan is defeated.

Prayer concerns God, and concerns man in every way. God has nothing too good to give in answer to prayer. There is no vengeance pronounced by God so dire which does not yield to prayer. There is no justice so flaming that is not quenched by prayer.

The possibilities of prayer are found in the illimitable promise, the willingness and the power of God to answer prayer, to answer all prayer, to answer every prayer, and to supply fully the illimitable need of man. None are so needy as man, none are so able and anxious to supply every need and any need as God.

Jesus Christ, this Divine man, died for all men. His life is but an intercession for all men. His death is but a prayer for all men. On earth, Jesus Christ knew no higher law, no holier business, no more divine life, than to plead for men. In heaven He knows no more royal estate, no higher theme, than to intercede for men. On earth He lived and prayed and died for men. His life, His death and His exaltation all plead for men.

Is there any work, higher work for the disciple to do than His Lord did? Is there any loftier employment, more honorable, more divine, than to pray for men? To take their woes, their sins, and their perils before God; to be one with Christ? To break the thrall which binds them, the hell which holds them, and lift them to immortality and eternal life?

In the example and the teaching of Jesus Christ, prayer assumes its normal relation to God's person, God's movements and God's Son. Jesus Christ was essentially the teacher of prayer by precept and example. We have glimpses of His praying which, like indices, tell how full of prayer the pages, chapters, and volumes of His life were. The epitome which covers not one segment only, but the whole circle of His life and character, is pre-eminently that of prayer!

"In the days of his flesh," the divine record reads, "when he had offered up prayers and supplications, with strong crying and tears. . . ." The suppliant of all suppliants He was, the intercessor of all intercessors. In lowliest form He approached God, and with strongest pleas He prayed and supplicated.

Jesus Christ teaches the importance of prayer by His urgency to His disciples to pray. But He shows us more than that. He shows how far prayer enters into the purposes of God. We must ever keep in mind that the relation of Jesus Christ to God is the relation of asking and giving; the Son ever asking, the Father ever giving. We must never forget that God has put the conquering, inheriting, and expanding forces of Christ's cause in prayer. "Ask of me, and I will give thee the heathen for thine inheritance, and the uttermost parts of the earth for thy possession."

Christ puts prayer among the statutory promises. He does not leave it to natural law. The law of need, demand and supply, of helplessness, of natural instincts, or the law of sweet, high, attractive privilege—these howsoever strong as motives of action, are not the basis of praying. Christ puts it as spiritual law. Men must pray. Not to pray is not simply a privation, an omission, but a positive violation of law, of spiritual life, a crime, bringing disorder and ruin. Prayer is law world-wide and eternity-reaching.

The teaching of Jesus Christ on the nature and necessity of prayer as recorded in His life, is remarkable. He sends men to their closets. *Prayer must be a holy exercise, untinted by vanity or pride. It must be in secret.* The disciple must live in secret. God lives there, is sought there, and is found there. The command of Christ as to prayer is that pride and publicity should be shunned. Prayer is to be in private. "But thou, when thou prayest, enter into thy closet, and shut thy door, and pray to thy Father in secret. And thy Father, which seeth in secret, shall reward thee openly."

From praying, Christ eliminates all self-sufficiency, all pride and all spiritual values. The poor in spirit are the praying ones. Beggars are God's princes. They are God's heirs. Christ removed the rubbish of Jewish traditions and glosses from the regulations of the prayer altar.

He who essays to pray to God with an angry spirit, with loose and irreverent lips, with an unreconciled heart, and with unsettled neighborly scores, spends his labor for that which is worse than nought, violates the law of prayer, and adds to his sin.

Praying must be done; God wants it done. He commands it, man needs it, and man must do it. Something must surely come of praying, for God engages that something shall come out of it, if men are in earnest and are persevering in prayer.

After Jesus teaches "ask and it shall be given you," He encourages real praying and more praying. He repeats and avers with redoubled assurance, "For everyone that asketh receiveth." No exceptions. "Everyone." "He that seeketh findeth." Here it is again, sealed and stamped with infinite veracity. Then closed and signed, as well as sealed, with divine attestation, "To him that knocketh it shall be opened."

Note how we are encouraged to pray by our relation to God! "If ye then, being evil, know how to give good gifts unto your children, how much more shall your Father which is in heaven give good things to them that ask him."

Luke tells us that as Jesus was praying in a certain place, when He ceased, one of His disciples said unto Him, "Lord, teach us to pray." This disciple had heard Jesus preach, but did not feel like saying, "Lord, teach us to preach." He could learn to preach by studying the methods of the Master. But there was something about the praying of Jesus that made the disciple feel like he did not know how to pray, that he had never prayed, and that he could not learn by listening even to the Master as He prayed. There is a profound something about prayer which never lies upon the surface. To learn it, one must go to the depths of the soul, and climb to the heights of God.

This Divine teacher of prayer lays himself out to make it clear and strong that God answers prayer, assuredly, certainly, inevitably; that it is the duty of the child to ask, and to press, and that the Father is obliged to answer, and to give for the asking. In Christ's teaching, prayer is no sterile, vain performance, not a mere rite, a form, but a request for an answer, a plea to gain, the seeking of a great good from God. It is a lesson of getting that for which we asked, of finding that for which we seek, and of entering the door at which we knock.

Fruit-bearing our Lord puts to the front in our praying: "Ye have not chosen me, but I have chosen you, and ordained you, that ye should go and bring forth fruit, and that your fruit should remain: that whatsoever ye shall ask of the Father in my name, he may give it you." Barrenness cannot pray. Fruit-bearing capacity and reality only can pray. It is not past fruitfulness, but present: "that your fruit should remain." Fruit, the product of life, is the condition of praying. A life vigorous enough to bear fruit, much fruit, is the condition and the source of prayer. "And in that day ye shall ask me nothing. Verily, verily, I say unto you, Whatsoever ye shall ask the Father in my name, he will give it you. Hitherto have ye asked nothing in my name: ask, and ye shall receive, that your joy may be full." "In that day ye shall ask me nothing."

It is not solving riddles, not revealing mysteries, not curious questioning. This is not our attitude, not our business under the dispensation of the Spirit, but to pray, and to pray largely. Much true praying increases man's joy and God's glory.

"As he was praying," so we are to be praying. If we would pray as Christ prayed, we must be as Christ was, and must live as Christ lived. The Christ character, the Christ life, and the Christ spirit, must be ours if we would do the Christ praying, and would have our prayers answered as He had His prayers answered. The business of Christ even now in heaven at His Father's right hand is to pray. Certainly if we are His, if we love Him, if we live for Him, and if we live close to Him, we will catch the contagion of His praying life, both on earth and in heaven. We will learn His trade and carry on His business on earth.

Jesus Christ loved all men, He tasted death for all men, He intercedes for all men. Let us ask then, Are we the imitators, the representatives, and the executors of Jesus Christ? Then must we in our prayers run parallel with His atonement in its extent. The atoning blood of Jesus gives sanctity and efficiency to our prayers. As world-wide, as broad, and as human as the man Christ Jesus was, so must be our prayers. The intercession of Christ's people must give currency and expedition to the work of Christ, carrying the atoning blood to its benignant ends, and help to strike off the chains to sin from every ransomed soul. We must be as praying, as tearful, and as compassionate as was Christ.

The praying of Christ was real. No man prayed as He prayed. Prayer pressed upon Him as a solemn, all-imperative, all-commanding duty, as well as a royal privilege in which as sweetness was condensed, alluring and absorbing. Prayer was the secret of His power, the law of His life, the inspiration of His toil, and the source of His wealth, His joy, His communion and strength. To Christ Jesus prayer occupied no secondary place, but was exacting and paramount, a necessity, a life, the satisfying of a restless yearning, and a preparation for heavy responsibilities.

Closeting with His Father in council and fellowship, with vigour and indeed joy, all this was His praying. Present trials, future glory, the history of His Church, and the struggles and perils of His disciples in all times and to the very end of time—all these things were born and shaped by His praying. Nothing is more conspicuous in the life of our Lord than prayer.

Paul gives in a brief and comprehensive statement the habit of our Lord in prayer in Hebrews 5:7: "Who, in the days of his flesh, when he had offered up prayers and supplications, with strong crying and tears, unto him that was able to save him from death, and was heard in that he feared." We have in this description of our Lord's praying the outgoing of great spiritual forces. He prayed with "prayers and supplications." It was no formal, tentative effort. He was intense, personal and real. He was a pleader for God's good. He was in great need and He must cry with "strong cryings," made stronger still by His tears. In an agony the Son of God wrestled. His praying was no playing a mere part. His soul is engaged, and all His powers were taxed to a strain. Let us pause and look at Him and learn how to pray in earnest. Let us learn how to win in an agony of prayer that which seems to be withholden from us. A beautiful word is that word "feared," which occurs only twice in the New Testament, the fear of God.

Jesus Christ was always a busy man, but never too busy to pray. "The divinest of business filled His heart and filled His hands, consumed His time, exhausted His nerves. *But with Him even God's work must not crowd out God's praying.* Saving people from sin or suffering must not, even with Christ, be substituted for praying, nor abate in the least the time or the intensity of these holiest of seasons. He filled the day with working for God; He employed the night with praying to God. The day-working made the night-praying a necessity. The night-praying sanctified and made successful the day-working. Too busy to pray gives religion Christian burial, it is true, but kills it nevertheless."

The prayer words of Jesus were sacred words. By them God speaks to God, and by them God is revealed and prayer is illustrated and enforced. Here is prayer in its purest form and in its mightiest potences. It would seem that earth and heaven would uncover head and open ears most wide to catch the words of His praying who was truest God and truest man, and divinest of suppliants, who prayed as never man prayed. His prayers are our inspiration and pattern to pray.

So he who follows Christ in prayer must have God's will and His law, His rule and His inspiration.

In all praying, it is the man who prays. The life
and the character flow into the closet.

There is mutual action and reaction. The closet
has much to do with making the character, while the
character has much to do with making the closet.
It is "the effectual, fervent prayer of a righteous man
[which] availeth much." It is with them who "call upon
the Lord out of a pure heart" who are to come forth.
Christ was the greatest of pray-ers because He was the
holiest of men. His character is the praying character.
His Spirit is the life and power of prayer. He is not
the best pray-er who has the greatest fluency, the most
brilliant imagination, the richest gifts, and the most
fiery ardor, but he who has imbibed most of the Spirit
of Christ.

The condition of receiving God's revelation and
of holding God's truth is one of the heart, not one of
the head. The ability to receive and search out is
like that of the child, the babe, the synonym of docility,
innocence and simplicity. These are the conditions on
which God reveals himself to men. The world by
wisdom cannot know God. The world by wisdom can
never receive nor understand God, because God reveals
himself to men's hearts, not to their heads. Only
hearts can ever know God, and feel God, can see
God, and can read God in His Book of books. God
is not grasped by thought but by feeling. The world
gets God by revelation, not by philosophy. It is not
apprehension, the mental ability to grasp God, but
plasticity, ability to be impressed, that men need. It is
not by hard, strong, stern, great reasoning that the
world gets God or that the world gets a hold of God,

but by big, soft, pure hearts. Not so much do men need light to see God as they need hearts to feel God.

Present in all great praying, making and marking it, is the man. It is impossible to separate the praying from the man. The constituent elements of the man are the constituents of his praying. The man flows through his praying. Only the fiery Elijah could do Elijah's fiery praying. We can get holy praying only from a holy man. Holy being can never exist without holy doing. Being is first, doing comes afterward. What we are gives being, force and inspiration to what we do. Character, that which is graven deeply, inerradicably, imperishably within us, colors all we do.

Christ led the way in prayer that we might follow His footsteps. Matchless leader in matchless praying! Lord, teach us to pray as thou didst Thyself pray! How marked the contrast between the sacerdotal prayer and this "Lord's Prayer," this copy for praying He gave to His disciples as the first elements of prayer. How simple and childlike! No one has ever approached in composition a prayer so simple in its petitions and yet so comprehensive in all of its requests and the personification.

How these simple elements of prayer as given by our Lord commend themselves to us! This prayer is for us as well as for those to whom it was first given— it for the child in the ABC of prayer, and it for the graduate of the highest institutions of learning. It is a personal prayer, reaching to all our needs and covering all our sins. It is the highest form of prayer for others. As the scholar can never in all his after-

studies or learning dispense with his ABC's, and as
the alphabet gives form, color and expression to all
after-learning, so all the learning in Christ can never
dispense with the Lord's Prayer. But he may make it
form the basis of his higher praying, this intercession for
others in the sacerdotal prayer. "In the reality of prayer
He sends them into the world just as His Father sent
Him into the world. He expects them to be and do just as
He was and did for His Father. He sought the sanctification of His disciples that they might be wholly devoted
to God and purified from all sin. He desired in them
a holy life and a holy work for God. He devoted
himself to death in order that they might be devoted in
life to God. For a true sanctification He prayed—a real,
whole, and thorough sanctification, embracing soul,
body and mind, for time and eternity. With Him
the Word itself had much to do with their true sanctification. "Sanctify them through thy truth: thy word
is truth. And for their sakes I sanctify myself, that
they also might be sanctified through the truth." Entire
devotedness was to be the type of their sanctification.
His prayer for their sanctification marks the pathway
to full sanctification. Prayer is that pathway. All the
ascending steps to that lofty position of entire sanctification are steps of prayer, increasing prayerfulness
in spirit and increasing prayerfulness in fact. "Pray
without ceasing" is the imperative prelude to "The
very God of peace sanctify you wholly." And prayer
is but the continued interlude and doxology of this
rich grace in the heart: "I pray God your whole spirit
and soul and body be preserved blameless unto the
coming of our Lord Jesus Christ. Faithful is he that
calleth you, who also will do it."

We can only meet our full responsibilities and fulfill our high mission when we go forth sanctified as Christ our Lord was sanctified. He sends us into the world just as His Father sent Him into the world. He expects us to be as He was, to do as He did, and to glorify the Father just as He glorified the Father.

The prayer in Gethsemane is exceptional in every way. The super-incumbent load of the world's sin is upon Him. The lowest point of His depression has been reached. The bitterest cup of all, His bitter cup, is being pressed to His lips. The weakness of all His weaknesses, the sorrow of all His sorrows, the agony of all His agonies is now upon Him. The flesh is giving out with its fainting and trembling pulsations, like the trickling of His heart's blood. His enemies have thus far triumphed. Hell is in jubilee and bad men are joining in the hellish carnival.

Gethsemane was Satan's hour, Satan's power, and Satan's darkness. It was the hour of forming all of Satan's forces for a final, last conflict. Jesus had said, "The prince of this world cometh and findeth nothing in me." The conflict for earth's mastery is before him.

The Spirit led and drove Him into the stern conflict and severe temptation of the wilderness. But His Comforter, His leader and His inspiration through history, seems to have left Him now. "He began to be sorrowful and very heavy," and we hear Him under this great pressure exclaiming, "My soul is exceeding sorrowful, even unto death." The depression, conflict and agony had gone to the very core of His Spirit, and had sunk into the verge of death. "Sore amazed" He was. Surprise and awe depress His soul. "Very heavy" was the hour of hell's midnight which fell upon His Spirit. Very heavy was this hour when all the sins of all the world, of every man, of all men, fell upon His immaculate soul, with all their stain and all their guilt.

He cannot abide the presence of His chosen friends. They cannot enter into the depth and demands of this fearful hour. His trusted and set watchers were asleep. His Father's face was hid. His Father's approving voice is silent. The Holy Spirit, who had been with Him through all the trying hours of His life, seems to have withdrawn from the scene. Alone He must drink the cup, alone He must tread the wine press of God's fierce wrath and of Satan's power and darkness, and of man's envy, cruelty and vindictiveness.

Nowhere in prophet or priest, king or ruler, of synagogue or church, does the ministry of prayer assume such marvels of variety, power and fragrance as in the life of Jesus Christ. It is the aroma of God's sweetest spices, a flame with God's glory, and consumed by God's will.

Christ was one with God's plan, and one with God's will. To pray in conformity with God's will was the life and law of Christ. The same was law of His praying. Conformity, to live one with God, is a far higher and more divine life than to live simply in submission to God. To pray in conformity—together with God—is a far higher and more divine way to pray than mere submission. At its best stage, submission is non-rebellion, an acquiescence, which is good, but not the highest. The most powerful form of praying is positive, aggressive, mightily outgoing and creative. It molds things, changes things, and brings things to pass.

Conformity means to "stand perfect and complete in all the will of God." It means to delight to do God's will, to run with eagerness and ardor to carry out His plans. Conformity to God's will involves submission—patient, loving, and sweet submission. But submission in itself falls short of and does not include conformity. We may be submissive but not conformed. We may accept results against which we have warred, and even be resigned to them.

Conformity means to be one with God, both in result and in processes. Submission may be one with God in the end. Conformity is one with God in the beginning, and the end. Jesus had conformity, absolute and perfect, to God's will, and by that He prayed.

We are ever ready to excuse our lack of earnest and toilsome praying by a fancied and delusive view of submission. We often end praying just where we ought to begin. We quit praying when God waits and is waiting for us to really pray. We are deterred by obstacles from praying, or we submit to difficulties and call it submission to God's will.

A world of beggarly faith, of spiritual laziness, and of half-heartedness in prayer, are covered under the high and pious name, submission. To have no plan but to see God's plan and carry it out, is of the essence and inspiration of Christly praying. This is far more than putting in a clause of submission. Jesus did this once in seeking to change the purpose of God, but all His other praying was the output of being perfectly one with the plans and purposes of God. It is after this order we pray when we abide in Him and when His Word abides in us. Then we ask what we will and it is done. It is then our prayers fashion and create things. Our wills then become God's will and His will becomes ours. The two become one, and there is not a note of discord.

What restraint, forbearance, self-denial, and loyalty to duty to God, and what difference to the Old Testament are in that statement of our Lord: "Thinkest thou that I cannot now pray to my Father, and he shall presently give me more than twelve legions of angels? But how then shall the scriptures be fulfilled, that thus it must be?"

During the great Welsh revival a minister was said to be very successful in winning souls by one sermon that he preached—hundreds were converted. Far away in a valley the news reached a brother minister of the marvelous success of this great sermon. He desired to find out the secret of the man's great success. He walked the long way and came to the minister's poor cottage, and the first thing he said was: "Brother, where did you get that sermon?" He was taken into a poorly furnished room and pointed to a spot where the carpet was worn threadbare, near a window that looked out upon the everlasting hills and solemn mountains and said, "Brother, there is where I got that sermon. My heart was heavy for men. One night I knelt there—and cried for power as I never preached before. The hours passed until midnight struck, and the stars looked down on a sleepy world, but the answer came not. I prayed on until I saw a faint streak of grey shoot up, then it was silver—then the silver became purple and gold. Then the sermon came and the power came and men fell under the influence of the Holy Spirit."—G. C. Morgan

How complex, confusing and involved is many a human direction about obtaining the gift of the Holy Spirit as the abiding Comforter, our sanctifier and the one who empowers us! How simple and direct is our Lord's direct—"ask"! This is plain and direct. Ask with urgency, ask without fainting. Ask, seek, knock, till He comes. Your heavenly Father will surely send Him if you ask for Him. Wait on the Lord for the Holy Spirit. It is the child waiting, asking, urging and praying perseveringly for the Father's greatest gift and for the child's greatest need, the Holy Ghost.

How are we to obtain the Holy Spirit so freely promised to those who seek Him believingly? Wait, press, and persevere with all the calmness and with all the ardor of a faith which knows no fear, which allows no doubt, a faith which staggers not at the promise through unbelief, a faith which in its darkest and most depressed hours against hope believes in hope, which is brightened by hope and strengthened by hope, and which is saved by hope.

Wait and pray—here is the key which unlocks every castle of despair, which opens every treasure-store of God. It is the simplicity of the child's asking of the Father who gives with a largeness, liberality, and cheerfulness, infinitely above anything ever known to earthly parents. Ask for the Holy Spirit—seek for the Holy Spirit—knock for the Holy Spirit. He is the Father's greatest gift for the child's greatest need.

In these three words, "ask," "seek," and "knock," given us by Christ, we have the repetition of the advancing steps of insistency and effort. He is laying himself out in command and promise in the strongest way, showing us that if we will lay ourselves out in prayer and will persevere, rising to higher and stronger attitudes and sinking to deeper depths of intensity and effort, the answer must inevitably come. So that it is true the stars would fail to shine before the asking, the seeking, and the knocking would fail to obtain what is needed and desired.

Our spirits are so fully indwelt by the Spirit of God, so responsive and obedient to His illumination and to His will, that we ask with holy boldness and freedom the things which the Spirit of God has shown us as the will of God, and faith is assured. Then "we know that we have the petitions that we have asked." The natural man prays, but prays according to his own will, fancy and desire. If he has ardent desires and groanings, they are the fire and agony of nature simply, and not that of the Spirit. What a world of natural praying there is, which is selfish, self-centered, self-inspired—the Spirit when He prays through us, or helps us to meet the mighty "oughtness" of right praying, trims our praying down to the will of God, and then we give heart and expression to His unutterable groanings. Then we have the mind of Christ, and pray as He would pray. His thoughts, purposes and desires are our desires, purposes and thoughts.

We are charged to supplicate in the Spirit and to pray in the Holy Spirit. We are reminded the Holy Spirit "helpeth our infirmities," and that while intercession is an art of so divine and so high a nature that though we know not what to pray for as we ought, yet the Spirit teaches us this heavenly science, by making intercession in us "with groanings which cannot be uttered." How burdened this intercession of the Holy Spirit! How profoundly He feels the world's loss, and how deeply He sympathizes with the dire conditions, are seen in His groanings which are too deep for utterance and too sacred to be voiced by Him. He inspires us to this most divine work of intercession and His strength enables us to sigh unto God for the oppressed, the burdened, and the distressed condition. The Holy Spirit helps us in many ways.

To pray by the Holy Spirit we must have Him always. He does not, like earthly teachers, teach us the lesson and then withdraw. He stays to help us practice the lesson He has taught. We pray, not by the precepts and the lessons He has taught, but *we pray by Him*. He is both teacher and lesson. We can only know the lesson because He is ever with us to inspire, to illumine, to explain, to help us to do. We pray not by the truth the Holy Spirit reveals to us, but *we pray by the actual presence of the Holy Spirit. He puts the desire in our hearts; kindles that desire by His own flame.* We simply give lip and voice and heart to His unutterable groanings. Our prayers are taken up by Him and energized and sanctified by His intercession. He prays for us, through us and in us. We pray by Him, through Him and in Him. He puts the prayer in us and we give it utterance and heart.

The Holy Spirit is the divinely appointed substitute for and representative of the personal and humanized Christ. How much is He to us! And how we are to be filled by Him, live in Him, walk in Him, and be led by Him! How we are to conserve and kindle to brighter and more consuming glow the holy flame! How careful should we be never to quench that pure flame! How watchful, tender, loving ought we to be so as not to grieve His sensitive, loving nature! How attentive, meek and obedient, never to resist His divine impulses, always to hear His voice, and always to do His divine will. How can all this be done without much and continuous prayer.

Prayer is the only element in which the Holy Spirit can live and work. Prayer is the golden chain which happily enslaves Him to His happy work in us.

Purpose
In Prayer

The prayers of holy men appease God's wrath, drive away temptations, resist and overcome the devil, procure the ministry and service of angels, rescind the decrees of God.

Prayer cures sickness and obtains pardon; it arrests the sun in its course and stays the wheels of the chariot of the moon; it rules over all gods and opens and shuts the storehouses of rain; it unlocks the cabinet of the womb and quenches the violence of fire; it stops the mouths of lions and reconciles our suffering and weak faculties with the violence of torment and violence of persecution; it pleases God and supplies all our need.

—Jeremy Taylor

CHAPTER TWO

PURPOSE IN PRAYER

The more praying there is in the world the better the world will be, the mightier the force against evil everywhere. Prayer, in one phase of its operation, is a disinfectant and a preventive. It purifies the air; it controls the contagion of evil. Prayer is no fitful, short-lived thing. It is no voice crying unheard and unheeded in the silence. It is a voice which goes into God's ear and it lives as long as God's ear is open to holy pleas, as long as God's heart is alive to holy things. God shapes the world by prayer. Prayers are deathless. The lips that utter them may be closed in death, the heart that felt them may have ceased to beat, but the prayers live before God, and God's heart is set on them. Prayers outlive the lives of those who uttered them; outlive a generation, outlive an age, outlive a world.

That man is the most immortal who has done the most and the best praying. They are God's heroes, God's saints, God's servants, God's vicegerents.

A man can pray better because of the prayers of the past; a man can live holier because of the prayers of the past. The man of many and acceptable prayers has done the truest and greatest service to the incoming generation. The prayers of God's saints strengthen the unborn generation against the desolating waves of sin and evil. Woe to the generation of sons who find their censers empty of the rich incense of prayer, whose fathers have been too busy or too unbelieving to pray, and perils inexpressible and consequences untold are their unhappy heritage. Fortunate are they whose fathers and mothers have left them a wealthy patrimony of prayer.

The prayers of God's saints are the capital stock in heaven by which Christ carries on His great work upon earth. The great throws and mighty convulsions on earth are the results of these prayers. Earth is changed, revolutionized, angels move on more powerful, more rapid wing, and God's policy is shaped as the prayers are more numerous, more efficient.

It is true that the mightiest successes that come to God's cause are created and carried on by prayer. God's day of power! The angelic days of activity and power are when God's Church comes into its mightiest inheritance of mightiest faith and mightiest prayer. God's conquering days are when the saints have given themselves to mightiest prayer. When God's house on earth is a house of prayer, then God's house in heaven is busy and all potent in its plans and movements, then His earthly armies are clothed with the triumphs and spoils of victory and His enemies defeated on every hand.

God conditions the very life and prosperity of His cause on prayer. The condition was put in the very existence of God's cause in this world. "Ask of me" is the one condition God puts in the very advance and triumph of His cause. Men are to pray—pray for the advance of God's cause. Prayer puts God in full force in the world. To a prayerful man God is present in realized force; to a prayerful church God is present in glorious power, and the second Psalm is the divine description of the establishment of God's cause through Jesus Christ. All inferior dispensations have merged in the enthronement of Jesus Christ. God declares the enthronement of His Son. The nations are incensed with bitter hatred against His cause. God is described as laughing at their enfeebled hate. The Lord will laugh; the Lord will have them in derision. "Yet have I set my King upon my holy hill of Zion."

The secret of success in Christ's kingdom is the ability to pray. The one who can wield the power of prayer is the strong one, the holy one in Christ's kingdom. The most important lesson we can learn is how to pray.

Prayer is the key note of the most sanctified life, of the holiest ministry. He does the most for God who is the highest skilled in prayer. Jesus Christ exercised His ministry after this order.

The possibilities and necessity of prayer, its power and results are manifested in arresting and changing the purposes of God and in relieving the stroke of His power. Pharaoh himself was a firm believer in the possibilities and its ability to relieve. When staggering under the woeful curses of God, he pleaded with Moses to intercede for him. "Entreat the Lord for me," was his pathetic appeal four times repeated when the plagues were scourging Egypt. Four times were these urgent appeals made to Moses, and four times did prayer lift the dread curse from the hard king and his doomed land.

The blasphemy and idolatry of Israel in making the golden calf and declaring their devotions to it, was a fearful crime. The anger of God waxed hot and He declared that He would destroy the offending people.

The Lord was very wroth with Aaron also, and to Moses He said, "Let me alone that I may destroy them." But Moses prayed, and kept on praying; day and night he prayed forty days. He makes the record of his prayer struggle. "I fell down," he says, "before the Lord at the first forty days and nights; I did neither eat bread nor drink water because of your sins which ye sinned in doing wickedly in the sight of the Lord to provoke him to anger. For I was afraid of the anger and hot displeasure wherewith the Lord was hot against you to destroy you. But the Lord hearkened to me at this time also. And the Lord was very angry with Aaron to have destroyed him, and I prayed for him also at the same time." Men like Moses knew how to pray and to prevail in prayer. Their faith in prayer was no passing attitude that changed with the wind or with their own feelings and circumstances; it was a fact that God heard and answered, that His ear was ever open to the cry of His children, and that the power to do what was asked of Him was commensurate with His willingness. And thus these men, strong in faith and in prayer, "subdued kingdoms, wrought righteousness, obtained promises, stopped the mouths of lions, quenched the violence of fire, escaped the edge of the sword, from weakness were made strong, waxed mighty in war, turned to flight the armies of the aliens."

Everything then, as now, was possible to the men and women who knew how to pray. Prayer, indeed, opened the limitless storehouse, and God's hand withheld nothing. Prayer introduced those who practiced it into a world of privilege, and brought the strength and wealth of heaven down to the aid of finite man. What rich and wonderful power was theirs who had learned the secret of victorious approach to God! With Moses it saved a nation; with Ezra it saved a church.

Prayer is no laggard's work. When all the rich, spiced graces from the body of prayer have by labor and beating been blended and refined and intermixed, the fire is needed to unloose the incense and make its fragrance rise to the throne of God. The fire that consumes creates the spirit and life of the incense. Without fire prayer has no spirit; it is, like dead spices, for corruption and worms.

The casual, intermittent prayer is never bathed in this divine fire. For the man who thus prays is lacking in the earnestness that lays hold of God, determined not to let Him go until the blessing comes. "Pray without ceasing," counselled the great Apostle. That is the habit that drives prayer right into the mortar that holds the building stones together. "You can do more than pray after you have prayed," said the godly Dr. A. J. Gordon, "but you cannot do more than pray until you have prayed."

The story of every great Christian achievement is the history of answered prayer. "The greatest and the best talent that God gives to any man or woman in this world is the talent of prayer," writes Principal Alexander Whyte. "And the best usury that any man or woman brings back to God when He comes to reckon with them at the end of this world is a life of prayer. And those servants best put their Lord's money 'to the exchangers' who rise early and sit late, as long as they are in this world, ever finding out and ever following after better and better methods of prayer, and ever forming more secret, more stedfast, and more spiritually fruitful habits of prayer, till they literally 'pray without ceasing,' and till they continually strike out into new enterprises in prayer, and new achievements and new enrichments." It is only when the whole heart is gripped with the passion of prayer that the life-giving fire descends, for none but the earnest man gets access to the ear of God.

Ever are the prayers of holy men streaming up to God as fragrant as the richest incense. And God in many ways is speaking to us, declaring His wealth and our impoverishment. "I am the maker of all things, the wealth and glory are mine. *Command* ye me." We can do all things by God's aid, and can have the whole of His aid by asking. The gospel in its success and power depends on our ability to pray. The dispensations of God depend on man's ability to pray. We can have all that God has. *Command* ye me. This is no figment of the imagination, no idle dream, no vain fancy. The life of the Church is the highest life. Its office is to pray. Its prayer life is the highest life, the most odorous, the most conspicuous.

The statement by the Baptist philosopher, John Foster, contains the purest philosophy and the simple truth of God, for God has no force and demands no conditions but prayer. "More and better praying will bring the surest and readiest triumph to God's cause; feeble, formal, listless praying brings decay and death. The Church has its sheet-anchor in the closet; its magazine stores are there."

"I am convinced," Foster continues, "that every man who amidst his serious projects is apprized of his dependence upon God as completely as that dependence is a fact, will be impelled to pray and anxious to induce his serious friends to pray almost every hour. He will not without it promise himself any noble success anymore than a mariner would expect to reach a distant coast by having his sail spread in a stagnation of air. I have intimated my fear that it is visionary to expect an unusual success in human administration of religion unless there are unusual omens: now a most emphatical spirit of prayer would be such an omen; and the individual who should determine to try its last possible efficacy might probably find himself becoming a much more prevailing agent in his little sphere. And if the whole of the greater number of the disciples of Christianity were with an earnest and unalterable resolution of each to combine that heaven should not withhold one single influence which the very utmost of effort of conspiring and persevering supplication would obtain, it would be a sign that a revolution of the world was at hand."

Edward Payson, one of God's own, says of this statement of Foster, "Very few missionaries since the apostles, probably have tried the experiment. He who shall make the first trial will, I believe, effect wonders. Nothing that I could write, nothing that an angel could write, will be necessary to him who should make this trial." Conscious as we are of the importance of prayer, of its vital importance, yet we let the hours pass away as a blank and can only lament in death the irremediable loss. When we calmly reflect upon the fact that the progress of our Lord's kingdom is dependent upon prayer, it is sad to think that we give so little time to the holy exercise. Everything depends upon prayer, and yet we neglect it not only to our own spiritual hurt but also to the delay and injury of our Lord's cause upon earth. The forces of good and evil are contending for the world. If we would, we could add to the conquering power of the army of righteousness, and yet we are sealed, our hands hang listlessly by our side, and we jeopardize the very cause in which we profess to be deeply interested by holding back from the prayer chamber.

Prayer is the one prime, eternal condition by which the Father is pledged to put the Son in possession of the world. Christ prays through His people. Had there been importunate, universal and continuous prayer by God's people, long ere this earth had been possessed for Christ. The delay is not to be accounted for by the inveterate obstacles, but the lack of the right asking. *We do more of everything else than of praying.* As poor as our giving is, our contributions of money exceed our offerings of prayer. Perhaps in the average congregation fifty aid in paying, where one saintly, ardent soul shuts itself up with God and wrestles for the deliverance of the heathen world. Official praying on set or state occasions counts for nothing in this estimate. We emphasize other things more than we do the necessity of prayer. John Foster puts the whole matter to a practical point. "When the Church of God," he says, "is aroused to its obligation and duties and right faith to claim what Christ had promised—'all things whatsoever'—a revolution will take place."

But not all praying is praying. The driving power, the conquering force in God's cause is God himself. "Call upon me and I will answer thee and show thee great and mighty things which thou knowest not," is God's challenge to prayer. Prayers puts God in full force into God's work. "Ask of me things to come, concerning my sons, and concerning the work of my hands command ye me"—God's *carte blanche* to prayer. *Faith is only omnipotent when on its knees,* and its outstretched hands take hold of God, then it draws to the utmost of God's capacity; for only a praying faith can get God's "all things whatsoever."

Our paucity in results, the cause of our leanness, is solved by the Apostle James—"Ye have not, because ye ask not. Ye ask and receive not because ye ask amiss, that ye may spend it on your pleasures." That is the whole truth in a nutshell. One of Melancthon's correspondents writes of Luther's praying: "I cannot enough admire the extraordinary cheerfulness, consistency, faith and hope of the man in these trying and

vexatious times. He constantly feeds these gracious
affections by a very diligent study of the Word of
God. *Then not a day passes in which he does not employ
in prayer at least three of his very best hours.* Once
I happened to hear him at prayer. Gracious God!
What spirit and what faith is there in his expressions!
He petitions God with as much reverence as if he
were in the divine presence, and yet with as firm
a hope and confidence as he would address a father
or a friend. 'I know,' said he, 'Thou art our Father and
our God; and therefore I am sure that Thou wilt bring to
nought the persecutors of Thy children. For shouldest
Thou fail to do this, Thine own cause, being connected
with ours, would be endangered. It is entirely Thine
own concern. We, by Thy providence, have been
compelled to take a part. Thou therefore wilt be our
defense.' *Whilst I was listening to Luther pray in this
manner, at a distance, my soul seemed on fire within
me,* to hear the man address God so like a friend, yet
with so much gravity and reverence; and also to hear
him, in the course of his prayer, insisting on the
promises contained in the Psalms, as if he were sure
his petitions would be granted."

"I tell the Lord my troubles and difficulties, and
wait for Him to give me the answers to them," said
one man of God. "And it is wonderful how a matter
that looked very dark will in prayer become clear as
crystal by the help of God's Spirit. I think Christians
fail so often to get answers to their prayers because
they do not wait long enough on God. They just drop
down and say a few words, and then jump up and forget it and expect God to answer them. Such praying
always reminds me of the small boy ringing his

neighbor's doorbell, and then running away as fast
as he can go."

Prayer is the easiest and the hardest of all things;
the simplest and the sublimest; the weakest and the
most powerful; its results lie outside the range of human
possibilities—they are limited only by the omnipotence
of God. *Few Christians have anything but a vague
idea of the power of prayer; fewer still have any experience of that power.* The Church seems almost wholly
unaware of the power God puts into her hand; this
spiritual carte blanche on the infinite resources of God's
wisdom and power is rarely, if ever, used—never used
to the full measure of honoring God. It is astounding
how poor the use, how little the benefits. Prayer is
our most formidable weapon, but the one in which we
are the least skilled, the most averse to its use. We
do everything else for the heathen save the thing
God wants us to do; the only thing which does any
good—makes all else we do efficient.

To graduate in the school of prayer is to master
the whole course of religious life. The first and last
stages of holy living are crowned with praying. It is
a life trade. The hindrances of prayer are the hindrances in the holy life. The conditions of praying
are the conditions of righteousness, holiness and salvation. A cobbler in the trade of praying is a bungler
in the trade of salvation.

Prayer is a trade to be learned. *We must be ap-
prentices* and serve our time at it. Painstaking care,
much thought, practice and labor are required to be
a skillful tradesman in praying. Practice in this as well

as in all other trades, makes perfect. Toiling hands and hearts only make proficients in this heavenly trade.

Prayer and a holy life are one. They mutually act and react. Neither can survive alone. The absence of the one is the absence of the other. The monks depraved prayer, substituted superstition for praying, mummeries and routine for a holy life. We are in danger of substituting churchly work and a ceaseless round of showy activities for prayer and holy living. *A holy life does not live in the closet, but it cannot live WITHOUT the closet.* If, by any chance, a prayer chamber should be established without a holy life, it would be a chamber without the presence of God in it.

More praying will not come as a matter of course. The campaign for the twentieth or thirtieth century will not help our praying, but hinder if we are not careful. Nothing but a specific effort from a praying leadership will avail. None but praying leaders can have praying followers. Praying apostles will beget praying saints. A praying pulpit will beget praying pews. We do greatly need somebody who can set the saints to this business of praying. *We are a generation of non-praying saints.* Non-praying saints are a beggarly gang of saints who have neither the ardor nor the beauty nor the power of saints. Who will restore this branch? *The greatest will he be of reformers and apostles, who can set the Church to praying.*

Holy men have in the past changed the whole force of affairs, revolutionized character and country by prayer. And such achievements are still possible to us. The power is only wanting to be used. Prayer is but the expression of faith.

Prayer honors God; it dishonors self. It is man's plea of weakness, ignorance, want. A plea which heaven cannot disregard. God delights to have us pray.

Prayer is not the foe to work; it does not paralyse activity. It works mightily; prayer itself is the greatest work. It springs activity, stimulates desire and effort. Prayer is not an opiate but a tonic, it does not lull to sleep but arouses anew for action. The lazy man does not, will not, cannot pray, for prayer demands energy. Paul calls it a striving, an agony. With Jacob it was wrestling; with the Syrophoenician woman it was a struggle which called into play all the higher qualities of the soul, and which demanded great force to meet.

The closet is not an asylum for the indolent and worthless Christian. It is not a nursery where none but babes belong. It is the battlefield of the Church; its citadel; the scene of heroic and unearthly conflicts. The closet is the base of supplies for the Christian and the Church. Cut off from it there is nothing left but retreat and disaster. The energy for work, the mastery over self, the deliverance from fear, all spiritual results and graces, are much advanced by prayer. The difference between the strength, the experience, the holiness of Christians is found in the contrast in their praying.

Few, short, feeble prayers, always betoken a low spiritual condition. Men ought to pray much and apply themselves to it with energy and perseverance. Eminent Christians have been eminent in prayer.

The deep things of God are learned nowhere else. Great things for God are done by great prayers. He who prays much, studies much, loves much, works much, does much for God and humanity. The execution of the gospel, the vigour of faith, the maturity and excellency of spiritual graces wait on prayer.

Without continuance the prayer may go unanswered. Importunity is made up of the ability to hold on, to press on, to wait with unrelaxed and relaxable grasp, restless desire and restful patience. Importunate prayer is not an incident, but the main thing, not a performance but a passion, not a need but a necessity.

Prayer in its highest form and grandest success assumes the attitude of a wrestler with God. It is a contest, trial and victory of faith; a victory not secured from an enemy, but *from Him who tries our faith that He may enlarge it*: that tests our strength to make us stronger. Few things give such quickened and permanent vigor to the soul as a long exhaustive season of importunate prayer. It makes an experience, an epoch, a new calendar for the spirit, a new life to religion, a soldierly training. There is neither encouragement nor room in Bible religion for feeble desires, listless efforts, lazy attitudes; all must be strenuous, urgent, ardent. Inflamed desires, impassioned, unwearied insistence delight heaven. God would have His children incorrigibly in earnest and persistently bold in their efforts. Heaven is too busy to listen to half-hearted prayers or to respond to pop calls.

There is not the least doubt that much of our praying fails for lack of persistency. It is without the fire and strength of perseverance. Persistency is of the essence of true praying. It may not be always called into exercise, but it must be there as the reserved force. Too often we get fainthearted and quit praying at the point where we ought to begin. We let go at the very point where we should hold on strongest. Our prayers are weak because they are not impassioned by an unfailing and resistless will. God loves the importunate pleader, and sends him answers that would never have been granted but for the persistency that refuses to let go until the petition craved for is granted.

Prayer is not a meaningless function of duty to be crowded into the busy or the weary ends of the day, and we are not obeying our Lord's command when we content ourselves with a few minutes on our knees in the morning rush or late at night when the faculties, tired with the tasks of the day, call out for rest.

God is always within call, it is true; His ear is ever attentive to the cry of His child, but we can never get to know Him if we use the vehicle of prayer as we use the telephone—for a few words of hurried conversation. Intimacy requires development.

We can never know God as it is our privilege to know Him, by brief and fragmentary and unconsidered repetitions of intercession that are requests for personal favors and nothing more.

The study of the Word and prayer go together, and where we find the one truly practiced, the other is sure to be seen in close alliance. Remember Luther's maxim, "To have prayed well is to have studied well." Luther spent his best three hours in prayer; John Welch prayed seven or eight hours a day. Welch used to keep a plaid on his bed that he might wrap himself in when he rose during the night. Sometimes his wife found him on the ground, lying weeping. When she complained, he would say, "Oh, woman, I have the souls of three thousand to answer for, and I know not how it is with many of them." The people Welch exhorted and charged by saying, "Pray for your pastor. Pray for his body that he may be kept strong and spared many years. Pray for his soul, that he may be kept humble and holy, a burning and shining light. Pray for his ministry, that it may be abundantly blessed, that he may be anointed to preach good tidings, that there be no secret prayer without naming him before your God, no family prayer without carrying your pastor in your heart to God." "Two things," says his biographer, "he seems never to have ceased from—the cultivation of personal holiness and the most anxious efforts to win souls."

Little prayer is the characteristic of a backslidden age and of a backslidden church. Whenever there is little praying in the pulpit or in the pew, spiritual bankruptcy is imminent and inevitable. The cause of God has no commercial age, no cultured age, no age of education, no age of money. But He has one golden age, and that is the age of prayer. When its leaders are men of prayer, when prayer is the prevailing element of worship, like the incense giving continual fragrance to its service, then that cause of God will be triumphant.

"Natural ability and educational advantages do not figure as factors in this matter; but a capacity for faith, the ability to pray, the power of a thorough consecration, the ability of self-littleness, an absolute losing of one's self in God's glory and an ever-present and insatiable yearning and seeking after all the fullness of God. Men who can set the Church ablaze for God, not in a noisy, showy way, but with an intense and quiet heat that melts and moves everything for God."

The prayer chamber conserves our relation to God. It hems every raw edge; it tucks up every flowing and entangling garment; girds up every fainting loin. The sheet anchor holds not the ship more securely and safely than the prayer chamber holds to God. Satan has to break our hold, and close up our way to the prayer chamber ere he can break our hold on God or close up our way to heaven.

"Be not afraid to pray; to pray is right;
   Pray if thou canst with hope, but ever pray,
Though hope be weak or sick with long delay;
   Pray in the darkness if there be no light;
And if for any wish thou dare not pray
   Then pray to God to cast that wish away."

Paul, Luther, Wesley—what would these chosen ones of God be without the distinguishing and controlling element of prayer? They were leaders for God because they were mighty in prayer. They were not leaders because of brilliancy in thought, because exhaustless in resources, because of their magnificent culture or native endowment. but leaders because by the power of prayer they could command the power of God. Praying men means much more than men who say prayers; much more than men who pray by habit. It means men with whom prayer is a mighty force, an energy that moves heaven and pulls untold treasures on earth.

The world is coming into the church at many points and in many ways. It oozes in; it pours in; it comes in with brazen front or soft, insinuating disguise; it comes in at the top and comes in at the bottom; and percolates through many a hidden way.

For praying men and holy men we are looking— men whose presence in the church will make it like a censer of holiest incense flaming up to God. With God the man counts for everything. Rites, forms, organizations are of small moment; unless they are backed by the holiness of the man, they are offensive in His sight. "Incense is an abomination unto me; the new moons and sabbaths, the calling of assemblies I cannot away with; it is iniquity, even the solemn meeting."

Why does God speak so strongly against His own ordinances? Personal purity had failed. The impure man tainted all the sacred institutions of God and defiled them. God regards the man in so important a way as to put a kind of discount on all else. Men have built Him glorious temples and have striven and exhausted themselves to please God by all manner of gifts; but in lofty strain He has rebuked these proud worshippers and rejected their princely gifts. "Heaven is my throne and earth is my footstool: where

is the house that ye build unto me? And where is
the place of my rest? For all those things hath mine
hand made, and all those things hath been, saith the
Lord. He that killeth an ox is as if he slew a man; he
that sacrificeth a lamb, as if he cut off a dog's neck;
he that offereth an oblation, as if he offered swine's
blood; he that burneth incense as if he blessed an
idol." Turning away in disgust from these costly
and profane offerings, He declares: "But to this man
will I look, even to him that is poor and of a contrite
spirit, and trembleth at my word." This truth that
God regards the personal purity of the man is funda-
mental. The man and his spiritual character depreciate
as church ceremonials increase. The simplicity of
worship is lost in religious æsthetics, or in the gaudiness
of religious forms.

"One night alone in prayer," says Spurgeon, "might
make us new men, changed from poverty of soul to
spiritual wealth, from trembling to triumphing. We
have an example of it in the life of Jacob. Afore time
the crafty shuffler, always bargaining and calculating,
unlovely in almost every respect, yet one night in
prayer turned the supplanter into a prevailing prince,
and robed him with celestial grandeur. From that
night he lives on the sacred page as one of the nobility of
heaven. Could not we, at least now and then, in these
weary earth-bound years, hedge about a single night for
such enriching traffic with the skies? What, have we no
sacred ambition? Are we deaf to the yearnings of
divine love? Yet, my brethren, for wealth and for
science men will cheerfully quit their warm couches,
and cannot we do it now and again for the love of
God and the good of souls? Where is our zeal, our

gratitude, our sincerity? I am ashamed while I thus upbraid both myself and you. May we often tarry at Jabbok and cry with Jacob, as he grasped the angel—

> 'With thee all night I mean to stay,
> And wrestle till the break of day.'

"Surely, brethren, if we have given whole days to folly, we can afford a space for heavenly wisdom. Time was when we gave whole nights to chambering and wantonness, to dancing in the world's revelry; we did not tire then; we were chiding the sun that he rose so soon, and wishing the hours would lag a little while that we might delight in wilder merriment and perhaps deeper sin. Oh, wherefore, should we weary in heavenly employments? Why grow we weary when asked to watch with our Lord? Up, sluggish heart, Jesus calls thee! Rise and go forth to meet the heavenly Friend in the place where He manifests himself." We can never expect to grow in the likeness of our Lord unless we follow His example and give more time to communion with the Father. A revival of real praying would produce a spiritual revolution.

It may be said with emphasis that no lazy saint prays. Can there be a lazy saint? Can there be a prayer-less saint? Does not slack praying cut short sainthood's crown and kingdom? Can there be a cowardly soldier? Can there be a saintly hypocrite? Can there be virtuous vice? It is only when these impossibilities are brought into being that we then can find a prayerless saint.

To go through the motion of praying is a dull business, though not a hard one. To say prayers in a decent, delicate way is not heavy work. But to pray really, to pray till hell feels the ponderous stroke, to pray till the iron gates of difficulties are opened, till the mountains of obstacles are removed, till the mists are exhaled and the clouds are lifted, and the sunshine of a cloudless day brightens—this is hard work, but it is God's work and man's best labor. Never was the toil of hand, head and heart less spent in vain than when praying. It is hard to wait and press and pray, and hear no voice, but stay till God answers.

Prayer honors God, acknowledges His being, exalts His power, adores His providence, secures His aid.

A sneering half-rationalism cries out against devotion, that it does nothing but pray. But to pray well is to do all things well. If it be true that devotion does nothing but pray, then it does nothing at all. To do nothing but pray fails to do the praying, for the antecedent, coincident, and subsequent conditions of prayer are but the sum of all the energized forces of a practical, working piety.

Why do we not pray? What are the hindrances to prayer? This is not a curious nor a trivial question. It goes not only to the whole matter of our praying, but to the whole matter of our religion. Religion is bound to decline when praying is hindered. That which hinders praying, hinders religion. *He who is too busy to pray will be too busy to live a holy life.*

Other duties become pressing and absorbing and crowd out prayer. Choked to death, would be the coroner's verdict in many cases of dead praying, if an inquest could be secured on this dire, spiritual calamity. This way of hindering prayer becomes so natural, so easy, so innocent, that it comes on us all unawares. If we will allow our praying to be crowded out, it will always be done. Satan would rather we let the grass grow on the path to our prayer chamber than anything else. A closed chamber of prayer means gone out of business religiously, or what is worse, made an assignment and carrying on our religion in some other name than God's and to somebody else's glory.

One of Satan's wiliest tricks is to destroy the best by the good. Business and other duties are good, but we are so filled with these that they crowd out and destroy the best. Prayer holds the citadel for God, and if Satan can by any means weaken prayer, he is a gainer so far, and when prayer is dead the citadel is taken.

We must keep prayer as the faithful sentinel keeps guard with sleepless vigilance. We must not keep it half-starved and feeble as a baby, but we must keep it in giant strength.

Prayer is a rare gift, not a popular, ready gift. Prayer is not the fruit of natural talents; it is the product of faith, of holiness, of deeply spiritual character. Men learn to pray as they learn to love. Perfection in simplicity, in humility, in faith—these form its chief ingredients. Novices in these graces are not adepts in prayer.

We must live for God out of the closet if we would meet God in the closet. We must bless God by praying lives if we would have God's blessing in the closet. We must do God's will in our lives if we would have God's ear in the closet. We must listen to God's voice in public if we would have God listen to our voice in private. God must have our hearts out of the closet if we would have God's presence in the closet. If we would have God in the closet, God must have us out of the closet. There is no way of praying to God but by living to God.

Our praying to be strong must be buttressed by holy living. The name of Christ must be honored by our lives before it will honor our intercessions. *The life of faith perfects the prayer of faith.*

"Here is the secret of prevailing prayer, to pray under a direct inspiration of the Holy Spirit, whose petitions for us and through us are always according to the divine purpose, and hence certain of answer. Praying in the Holy Ghost is but cooperating with the will of God, and such prayer is always victorious. How many Christians there are who cannot pray, and who seek by efforts, resolve, joining prayer circles, etc., to cultivate in themselves the 'holy art of intercession,' and all to no purpose. Here for them and for all is the only secret of a real prayer life—'Be filled with the Spirit,' who is 'the Spirit of grace and supplication.' "
—Rev. J. Stuart Holden

The preceding chapter has stated that prayer can do anything that God can do. It is a tremendous statement to make, but is a statement born out by history and experience. If we are abiding in Christ—and if we abide in Him we are living in obedience to His

holy will—and approach God in His name, then there
lie before us the infinite resources of the divine treasure house. Prayer is not acting a part or going through
religious motions. Prayer is neither official nor formal
nor ceremonial, but direct, hearty, intense. The object
of asking is to receive. The aim of seeking is to find.
The purpose of knocking is to arouse attention and
get in, and this is Christ's iterated and reiterated as-
severation that the prayer without doubt will be answered; its end without doubt secured. Not by some
roundabout way, but by getting the very thing asked
for.

The value of prayer does not lie in the number of
prayers, nor in the length of prayers, but its value is
found in the great truth that we are privileged by
our relation to God to unburden our desires and make
requests known to God. and He will relieve by granting our petitions. The child asks because the parent
is in the habit of granting the child's requests. As the
children of God we need something and we need it
badly, and we go to God for it. Neither the Bible nor
the child of God knows anything of that half-infidel
declaration, that we are to answer our own prayers.
God answers prayer. The true Christian does not pray
to stir himself up, but his praying is the stirring up of
himself to take hold of God.

To the man or woman who is acquainted with God
and knows how to pray, there is nothing remarkable
in the answers that come. They are sure of being heard,
since they ask in accordance with what they know to
be the mind and the will of God. Dr. William Burt,
Bishop of Europe in the Methodist Episcopal Church.

tells that a few years ago when he visited their Boys'
School in Vienna, he found that although the year
was not up, all available funds had been spent. He
hesitated to make a special appeal to his friends in
America. He counselled with the teachers. They took
the matter to God in earnest and continued prayer,
believing that He would grant their request. Ten days
later Bishop Burt was in Rome, and there came to
him a letter from a friend in New York, which read
substantially thus: "As I went to my office on Broad-
way one morning [and the day was the very one on
which the teachers were praying], a voice seemed to
tell me that you were in need of funds for the Boys'
School in Vienna. I very gladly enclosed a check for
the work." *The check was for the amount needed.
There had been no human communication* between
Vienna and New York. But while they were yet speaking God answered them.

Every revival of which we have any record has
been bathed in prayer. Take, for example, the wonderful revival in Shotts (Scotland) in 1630. The fact that
several of the then persecuted ministers would take a
part in solemn convocation having become generally
known, a vast concourse of godly persons assembled
on this occasion from all quarters of the country, and
several days were spent in social prayer, preparatory
to the service. In the evening, instead of retiring to
rest, the multitude divided themselves into little bands,
and spent the whole night in supplication and praise.
The Monday was consecrated to thanksgiving, a practice not then common, and proved the great day of
the feast. After much entreaty, John Livingston,
chaplain to the Countess of Wigtown, a young man

and not ordained, agreed to preach. *He had spent the night in prayer* and conference—but as the hour of assembly approached, his heart quailed at the thought of addressing so many aged and experienced saints, and he actually fled from the duty he had undertaken. But just as the kirk of Shotts was vanishing from his view, these words, "Was I ever a barren wilderness or a land of darkness?" were borne in upon his mind with such force as compelled him to return to the work. He took for his text Ezekiel 36:25, 26, and discoursed with great power for about two hours. *Five hundred conversions* were believed to have occurred under that one sermon, thus prefaced by prayer.

Power
Through Prayer

We care not for your splendid abilities as a minister, or your natural endowment as an orator before men. We are sure that the truth of the matter is this: No one will or can command success and become a real praying soul unless intense application is the price. I am even now convinced that the difference between the saints like Wesley, Fletcher, Edwards, Brainerd, Bramwell, Bounds, and ourselves is energy, perseverance, invincible determination to succeed or die in the attempt, God help us.

—Homer W. Hodge

A certain preacher whose sermons converted many souls received a revelation from God that it was not his sermons or works by all means but the prayers of an illiterate lay brother who sat on the pulpit steps pleading for the success of the sermon. It may be in the all-revealing day so with us. We may believe after labouring long and wearily, that all honor belongs to another builder whose prayers were gold, silver, precious stones, while our sermonizings being apart from prayer are but hay and stubble.

—Charles Haddon Spurgeon

CHAPTER THREE

POWER THROUGH PRAYER

We are constantly on a stretch, if not on a strain, to devise new methods, new plans, new organizations to advance the Church and secure enlargement and efficiency for the gospel. This trend of the day has a tendency to lose sight of the man or sink the man in the plan or organization. God's plan is to make much of the man, far more of him than anything else. Men are God's method. The Church is looking for better methods; God is looking for better men.

What the church needs today is not more machinery or better, not new organizations or more and novel methods, but men whom the Holy Ghost can use— men of prayer, men mighty in prayer. The Holy Ghost does not flow through methods, but through men. He does not come on machinery, but on men. He does not anoint plans, but men—men of prayer.

The man makes the preacher. God must make the man. The messenger is, if possible, more than the message. The preacher is more than the sermon. The preacher makes the sermon. As the life-giving milk from the mother's bosom is but the mother's life, so all the preacher says is tinctured, impregnated by what the preacher is. The treasure is in earthen vessels and the taste of the vessel impregnates and may discolor. The man, the whole man, lies behind the sermon. Preaching is not the performance of an hour. It is the outflow of a life. It takes twenty years to make a sermon, because it takes twenty years to make the man. The true sermon is a thing of life. The sermon grows because the man grows. The sermon is forceful because the man is forceful. The sermon is holy because the man is holy. The sermon is full of the divine unction because the man is full of the divine unction.

The sermon cannot rise in its life-giving forces above the man. Dead men give out dead sermons, and dead sermons kill. Everything depends upon the spiritual character of the preacher. Under the Jewish dispensation the high priest had inscribed in dual letters on a golden frontlet: "Holiness unto the Lord." So every preacher in Christ's ministry must be molded into and mastered by this same holy motto. Jonathan Edwards said: "I went on with my eager pursuit after more holiness and more conformity to Christ. The heaven I desired was the heaven of holiness."

The constraining power of love must be in the preacher as a projecting, eccentric, all-commanding, self-oblivious force. The energy of self-denial must be his being, his heart and blood and bones. He must go forth as a man among men, clothed with humility, abiding in meekness, wise as a serpent, harmless as a dove; the bonds of a servant with the spirit of a king, a king in high, royal, independent bearing, with the simplicity and sweetness of a child. The preacher must throw himself, with all the abandon of a perfect, self-emptying faith and a self-consuming zeal, into his work for the salvation of men. Hearty, heroic, compassionate, fearless martyrs must the men be who take hold of and shape a generation for God. If they be timid time-servers, place-seekers; if they be men-pleasers or men-fearers; if their faith has a weak hold on God or His Word; if their denial be broken by any phase of self or the world, they cannot take hold of the Church nor the world for God.

The preacher's sharpest and strongest preaching should be to himself. His most difficult, delicate, laborious, thorough work must be with himself. The training of the twelve apostles was the great, difficult, and enduring work of Christ. Preachers are not sermon-makers, but men-makers, and saint-makers, and he only is well-trained for this business who has made himself a man and a saint. It is not great talents nor great learning nor great preachers that God needs but men great in holiness, great in faith, great in love, great in fidelity, great for God—men always preaching by holy sermons in the pulpit, by holy lives out of it. These can mold a generation for God.

The real sermon is made in the closet. The man—God's man—is made in the closet. His life and his profoundest convictions were born in his secret communion with God. The burdened and tearful agony of his spirit, his weightiest and sweetest messages were got when alone with God. Prayer makes the man; prayer makes the preacher; prayer makes the pastor.

The pulpit of this day is weak in praying. The pride of learning is against the dependent humility of prayer. Prayer is with the pulpit too often only official—a performance for the routine of service. Prayer is not to the modern pulpit the mighty force it was in Paul's life or Paul's ministry. Every preacher who does not make prayer a mighty factor in his own life and ministry is weak as a factor in God's work and is powerless to project God's cause in this world.

The preaching that kills is non-spiritual preaching. The ability of the preaching is not from God. Lower sources than God give to it energy and stimulant. The Spirit is not evident in the preacher nor in his preaching. Many kinds of forces may be projected and stimulated by *preaching that kills*, but they're not spiritual forces. *The preaching that kills* is the letter; shapely and orderly it may be, but it is the letter still, the dry, husky letter, the empty, bald shell. The letter may have the germ of life in it, but it has no breath of spring to evoke it.

Winter seeds they are, as hard as the winter's soil, as icy as the winter's air, no thawing nor germinating by them. This letter-preaching has the truth. But even divine truth has no life-giving energy alone; it must be energized by the Spirit, with all God's forces at its back. Truth unquickened by God's Spirit deadens as much as, or more than, error. It may be the truth without admixture; but without the Spirit its shade and touch are deadly, its truth error, its light darkness. The letter-preaching is unctionless, neither mellowed nor oiled by the Spirit. There may be tears, but tears cannot run God's machinery; tears may be but the summer's breath on a snow-covered iceberg, nothing but surface slush. Feelings and earnestness there may be, but it is the emotion of the actor and the earnestness of the attorney. The preacher may feel from the kindling of his own sparks, be eloquent over his own exegesis, earnest in delivering the product of his own brain; the professor may usurp the place and imitate the fire of the apostle; brains and nerves may serve the place and feign the work of God's Spirit, and by these forces the letter may glow and sparkle like an illumined text, but the glow and sparkle will be as barren of life as the field sown with pearls. The death-dealing element lies back of the words, back of the sermon, back of the occasion, back of the manner, back of the action.

The great hindrance is in the preacher himself. He has not in himself the mighty life-creating forces. There may be no discount on his orthodoxy, honesty, cleanness, or earnestness; but somehow the man, the inner man, in its secret places has never been broken down and surrendered to God, his inner life is not a great highway for the transmission of God's message, or God's power. Somehow self and not God rules in the holy of holies. Somewhere, all unconscious to himself, some spiritual non-conductor has touched his inner being, and the divine current has been arrested. His inner being has never felt its thorough spiritual bankruptcy, its utter powerlessness; he has never learned to cry out with an ineffable cry of self-despair and self-helplessness till God's power and God's fire comes in and fills, purifies, empowers. Self-esteem, self-ability in some pernicious shape has defamed and violated the temple which should be held sacred for God. *Life-giving preaching costs the preacher much—death to self,*

crucifixion to the world, the travail of his own soul.
Crucified preaching only can give life. *Crucified preaching can come only from a crucified man.*

The preaching that kills may be, and so often is, orthodox—dogmatically, inviolably orthodox. We love orthodoxy. It is good. It is the best. It is the clean, clear-cut teaching of God's Word, the trophies won by truth in its conflict with error, the levies which faith has raised against the desolating floods of honest or reckless misbelief or unbelief; but orthodoxy, clear, and hard as crystal, suspicious and militant, may be but the letter well-shaped, well-named, and well-learned, the letter which kills. Nothing is so dead as a dead orthodoxy, too dead to speculate, too dead to think, to study, or to pray.

The preaching that kills may have insight and grasp of principles, may be scholarly and critical in taste, may have every minutia of the derivation and grammar of the letter, may be able to trim the letter to its perfect pattern, and illuminate it as Plato and Cicero may be lumined, may study it as a lawyer studies his textbooks to form his brief or to defend his case, and yet be like a frost, a killing frost.

Letter-preaching may be eloquent, enamelled with poetry and rhetoric, sprinkled with prayer, spiced with sensation, illumined by genius, and yet these be but the massive or chaste costly mountings, the rare and beautiful flowers which coffin the corpse. *The preaching which kills* may be without scholarship, unmarked by any freshness of feeling or thought, clothed in tasteless generalities or vapid specialities,

with style irregular, slovenly, saving neither of closet
nor of study, graced neither by thought, expression, or
prayer. Under such preaching how wide and utter the
desolation—how profound the spiritual death!

Preaching that kills is prayerless preaching. Without prayer the preacher creates death, and not life.
The preacher who is feeble in prayer is feeble in life-
giving forces. The preacher who has retired prayer
as a conspicuous and largely prevailing element in
his own character has shorn his preaching of its
distinctive life-giving power. Professional praying there
is and will be, but professional praying helps the
preaching to its deadly work. Professional praying chills
and kills both preaching and praying. Much of the lax
devotion and lazy, irreverent attitudes in congregational
praying are attributable to professional praying in the
pulpit. Long, discursive, dry, and inane are the prayers
in many pulpits. Without unction or heart, they fall
like a killing frost on all the graces of worship. Death-
dealing prayers they are. Every vestige of devotion
has perished under their breath. The more dead they
are the longer they grow. A plea for short praying,
life praying, real heart praying, praying by the Holy
Spirit—direct, specific, ardent, simple, unctious in the
pulpit—is in order. A school to teach ministers how
to pray, as God counts praying, will be more beneficial
to true piety, true worship, and true preaching than
all theological schools.

Mr. Spurgeon says, "Of course the preacher is above
all others distinguished as a man of prayer. He prays
as an ordinary Christian, else he were a hypocrite. He
prays more than ordinary Christians, else he were

disqualified for the office he has undertaken. If you as a minister are not very prayerful, you ought to be pitied. If you become lax in sacred devotion, not only will you need to be pitied but your people also, and the day cometh in which you shall be ashamed and confounded. All our libraries and studies are mere emptiness compared with our closets. Our seasons of fasting and prayer at the Tabernacle have been high days indeed; never has heaven's gate stood wider, never have our hearts been nearer the central glory."

Prayer is not a little habit pinned on to us while we were tied to our mother's apron strings; neither is it a little decent quarter of a minute's grace said over an hour's dinner, but it is a most serious work of our most serious years. It engages more of time and appetite than our longest dinings or richest feasts. The prayer that makes much of our preaching must be made much of. The character of our praying will determine the character of our preaching. Light praying will make light preaching. Prayer makes preaching strong, gives it unction, and makes it stick. In every ministry weighty for good, prayer has always been a serious business.

The preacher must be pre-eminently a man of prayer. His heart must graduate in the school of prayer. In the school of prayer only can the heart learn to preach. No learning can make up for the failure to pray. No earnestness, no diligence, no study, no gifts will supply its lack.

Talking to men for God is a great thing, but talking to God for men is greater still. He will never talk well and with real success to men for God who has not learned well how to talk to God for men. More than this, prayerless words in the pulpit and out of it are deadening words.

Prayer, in the preacher's life, in the preacher's study, in the preacher's pulpit, must be a conspicuous and an all-impregnating force and an all-coloring ingredient. It must play no secondary part, be no mere coating. To him it is given to be with his Lord "all night in prayer." The preacher to train himself in self-denying prayer, is charged to look to his Master, who, "rising up a great while before day, went out, and departed into a solitary place, and there prayed." The preacher's study ought to be a closet, a Bethel, an altar, a vision, and a ladder, that every thought might ascend heavenward ere it went manward; that every part of the sermon might be scented by the air of heaven and be made serious, because God was in the study.

As the engine never moves until the fire is kindled, so preaching, with all its machinery, perfection, and polish, is at a dead standstill as far as spiritual results are concerned, till prayer has kindled and created the steam. The texture, fineness, and strength of the sermon is as so much rubbish unless the mighty impulse of prayer is in it, through it, and behind it. The preacher must, by prayer, put God in the sermon. The preacher must, by prayer, move God toward the people before he can move the people to God by his words. The preacher must have had audience and ready access to God before he can have access to the people. An open way to God for the preacher is the surest pledge of an open way to the people.

It is necessary to iterate and reiterate, that prayer, as a mere habit, as a performance gone through by routine or in a professional way, is a dead and rotten thing. Such praying has no connection with the praying for which we plead. We are stressing true praying, which engages and sets on fire every high element of the preacher's being—prayer which is born of vital oneness with Christ and the fullness of the Holy Ghost, which springs from the deep, overflowing fountains of tender compassion, deathless solicitude for man's eternal good; a consuming zeal for the glory of God, a further conviction of the preacher's difficult and delicate work and of the imperative need of God's mightiest help. Praying grounded on these solemn and profound convictions is the only true praying. Preaching backed by such praying is the only preaching which sows the seeds of eternal life in human hearts and builds men up for heaven.

The preachers who gain mighty results for God are the men who have prevailed in their pleadings with God ere venturing to plead with men. The preachers who are the mightiest in their closets with God are the mightiest in their pulpits with men.

Preachers are human folks, and are exposed to and often caught by the strong driftings of human currents. Praying is spiritual work; and human nature does not like taxing, spiritual work. Human nature wants to sail to heaven under a favoring breeze, a full, smooth sea. *Prayer is humbling work. It abases intellect and pride, crucifies vain glory, and signs our spiritual bankruptcy, and all these are hard for flesh and blood to bear*. It is easier not to pray than to bear them. So we come to one of the crying evils of these times, maybe of all times—little or no praying. Of these two evils, perhaps little praying is worse than no praying. Little praying is a kind of make-believe, a salve for the conscience, a farce and a delusion.

The preacher is commissioned to pray as well as to preach. His mission is incomplete if he does not do both well. The preacher may speak with all eloquence of men and of angels; but unless he can pray with a faith that draws all heaven to his aid, his preaching will be "as sounding brass or a tinkling cymbal" for permanent, God-honoring, soul-saving uses.

Prayer which is felt as a mighty force is the mediate or immediate product of much time spent with God. Our short prayers owe their point and efficiency to the long ones that have preceded them. The short prevailing prayer cannot be prayed by one who has not prevailed with God in a mightier struggle of long continuance. Jacob's victory of faith could not have been gained without that all-night wrestling. God's acquaintance is not made by pop calls. God does not bestow His gifts on the hasty comers and goers. Much with God alone is the secret of knowing Him and of influencing with Him. He yields to the persistency of a faith that knows Him.

The men who have most fully illustrated Christ in their character, and have most powerfully affected the world for Him, have been men who have spent so much time with God as to make it a notable feature in their lives.

Charles Simeon—devoted the hours from four to eight in the morning to God.

John Wesley—spent two hours daily in prayer. He began at four in the morning. Of him, one who knew him well wrote: "He thought prayer to be his business more than anything else, and I have seen him come out of his closet with a serenity of face next to shining."

John Fletcher—stained the walls of his room by the breath of his prayers. Sometimes he would pray all night; always, frequently, and with great earnestness. His whole life was a life of prayer. "I would not rise from my seat," he said, "without lifting my heart to God." His greeting to a friend was always; "Do I meet you praying?"

Martin Luther—said, "If I fail to spend two hours in prayer each morning, the devil gets the victory through the day. I have so much business I cannot get on without spending three hours daily in prayer." He had a motto: "He that has prayed well has studied well."

Archbishop Leighton—was so much alone with God that he seemed to be in perpetual meditation. "Prayer and praise were his business and his pleasure," says his biographer.

Bishop Ken—was so much with God that his soul was said to be God enamored. He was with God before the clock struck three every morning.

Bishop Asbury—said: "I propose to rise at four

o'clock as often as I can and spend two hours in prayer and meditation."

Samuel Rutherford—the fragrance of whose piety is still rich, rose at three in the morning to meet God in prayer.

Joseph Alleine—arose at four o'clock for this business of praying till eight. If he heard other tradesmen plying their business before he was up, he would exclaim: "Oh, how this shames me! Doth not my Master deserve more than theirs?"

He who has learned this trade well draws at will, on sight, and with acceptance of heaven's unfailing bank.

John Welch—the holy and wonderful Scottish preacher, thought the day illspent if he did not spend eight or ten hours in prayer.

Bishop Wilson—says: "In Henry Martyn's journal, the spirit of prayer, the time he devoted to the duty, and his fervor in it are the finest things which strike me."

Edward Payson—wore the hard-wood boards into grooves where his knees pressed so often and so long. His biographer says: "His continuing instant in prayer, be his circumstances what they might, is the most noticeable fact in his history, and points out the duty of all who would rival his eminency. To his ardent and persevering prayers must no doubt be ascribed in a great measure his distinguished and almost uninterrupted success."

The Marquis DeRenty—to whom Christ was most precious, ordered his servant to call him from his devotions at the end of half an hour. The servant at the time saw his face through an aperture. It was marked with such holiness that he hated to arouse him. His lips were moving, but he was perfectly silent. He waited until three half hours had passed; then he called to him. When he arose from his knees, he said that the half hour was so short when he was communing with Christ.

David Brainerd—said: "I love to be alone in my cottage, where I can spend much time in prayer."

William Bramwell—is famous in Methodist annals for personal holiness and for his wonderful success in preaching and for the marvelous answers to his prayers. For hours at a time he would pray. He almost lived on his knees. He went over his circuits like a flame of fire. The fire was kindled by the time he spent in prayer. He often spent as much as four hours in a single season of prayer in retirement.

Bishop Andrewes—spent the greatest part of five hours every day in prayer and devotion.

Sir Henry Havelock—always spent the first two hours of the day alone with God. If the encampment was struck at six a.m., he would rise at four.

Earl Cairns—rose daily at six o'clock to secure an hour and a half for the study of the Bible and for prayer before conducting family worship at a quarter to eight.

Adoniram Judson's—success in prayer is attributable to the fact that he gave much time to prayer. He says on this point: "Arrange thy affairs, if possible, so that thou canst leisurely devote two or three hours every day not merely to devotional exercises but to the very act of secret prayer and communion with God. Endeavor seven times a day to withdraw from business and company and lift thy soul to God in private retirement. Begin the day by rising after midnight and devoting some time amid the silence of darkness of the night to this sacred work. Let the hour of opening dawn find thee at the same work. Let the hours of nine, twelve, three, six, and nine at night witness the same. Be resolute in His cause. Make all practicable sacrifices to maintain it. *Consider that thy time is short, and that business and company must not be allowed to rob thee of thy God.*" Impossible, we say, fanaticable directions! Dr. Judson impressed an empire for Christ and laid the foundation of God's kingdom with imperishable granite in the heart of Burma. He was successful, one of the few men who mightily impressed the world for Christ. Many men have greater gifts and genius and learning and have made no such impression; their religious work is like footsteps in the sands, but he has engraven his work on the adamant.

Everywhere, everything in apostolic times was on the stretch that the people of God might each and "all come in the unity of the faith, and of the knowledge of the Son of God, unto a perfect man, unto the measure of the stature of the fulness of Christ." No premium was given to dwarfs; no encouragement to an old babyhood. The babies were to grow; the old, instead of feebleness and infirmities, were to bear fruit in old age, and be fat and flourishing. The most divine thing in religion is holy men and holy women.

No amount of money, genius, or culture can move things for God. Holiness energizing the souls, the whole man aflame with love, with desire for more faith, more prayer, more zeal, more consecration—this is the secret of power. These we need and must have, and men must be the incarnation of this God-inflamed devotedness. God's advance has been stayed, His cause crippled, His name dishonored for their lack. Genius (though the loftiest and most gifted), education (though the most learned and refined), position, dignity, place, honored names, high ecclesiastics cannot move this chariot of our God. It is a fiery one, and only fiery forces can move it. The genius of a Milton fails. The imperial strength of a Leo fails. Brainerd's spirit can move it. Brainerd's spirit was on fire for God, on fire for souls. Nothing earthly, worldly, selfish came in to abate in the least the intensity of this all-impelling and all-consuming force and flame. Prayer is the creator as well as the channel of devotion. The spirit of devotion is the spirit of prayer. Prayer and devotion are united as soul and body are, united, as life and heart are united. There is no real prayer without devotion, no devotion without prayer. The preacher must be surrendered to God in the holiest devotion. He is not a professional man, his ministry is not a profession; it is a divine institution, a divine devotion. The preacher, above everything else, must be devoted to God. The preacher's relations to God are the insignia and credentials of his ministry. They must be clear, conclusive, unmistakable. No common, surface type of piety must be his. If he does not excel in grace, he does not excel at all. If he does not preach by life, character, conduct, he does not preach at all. If his piety be light, his preaching may be as soft and as sweet as music, as gifted as Apollo, yet its weight will be a feather's weight, visionary, fleeting as the morning cloud or the early dew.

Never did the cause of God need perfect illustrations of the possibilities of prayer more than in this age. No age, no person, will be ensamples of the gospel power except the ages or persons of deep and earnest prayer. A prayerless age will have but scant models of divine power. Prayerless hearts will never rise to these Alpine heights. The age may be a better age than the past, but there is an infinite distance between the betterment of an age by the force of advancing civilization and its betterment by the increase of holiness and Christlikeness by the energy of prayer. The Jews were much better when Christ came than in the ages before. It was the golden age of their Pharisaic religion. Their golden religious age crucified Christ. Never more praying, never less praying; never more sacrifices, never less sacrifice; never more idolatry, never less idolatry; never more of temple worship, never less of God worship; never more of lip service, never less of heart service (God worship by lips whose hearts and hands crucified God's Son!); never more of church-goers, never less of saints.

It is a prayer-force which makes saints. Holy characters are formed by the power of real praying. The more of true saints, the more of true praying; the more of true praying, the more of true saints.

The men of mighty prayer are men of spiritual might. *Prayers never die.* Brainerd's whole life was a life of prayer. By day and by night he prayed. Before preaching and after preaching he prayed. Riding through the interminable solitudes of the forests he prayed. On his bed of straw he prayed. Retiring to the dense and lonely forests he prayed. Hour by hour, day after day, early morn and late at night, he was praying and fasting, pouring out his soul, interceding, communing with God. He was with God mightily in prayer, and God was with him mightily, and by it he being dead yet speaketh and worketh, and will speak and work till the end comes, and among the glorious ones of that glorious day he will be with the first.

Jonathan Edwards says of him; "His life shows the right way to success in the works of the ministry. He sought it as a soldier seeks victory in a siege or battle; or as a man who runs a race for a great prize. Animated with love to Christ and souls, how did he labor? Always fervently. Not only in words and doctrine, in public and in private, but in prayers by day and night, wrestling with God in secret and travailing in birth with unutterable groans and agonies, until Christ was formed in the hearts of the people to whom he was sent. Like a true son of Jacob, he persevered in wrestling all through the dark hours of the night, until the breaking of the day."

Prayer, with its manifold and many-sided forces, helps the mouth to utter the truth in its fullness and freedom. The preacher is to be prayed for. The preacher is made by prayer. The preacher's mouth is to be prayed for; his mouth is to be opened and filled by prayer. A holy mouth is made by praying, by much praying; a brave mouth is made by praying, by much praying. The Church and the world, God and heaven, owe much to Paul's mouth; Paul's mouth owed its power to prayer.

How manifold, illimitable, valuable, and helpful prayer is to the preacher in so many ways, at so many points, in every way! One great value is, it helps his heart. Praying makes the preacher a heart-preacher. Prayer puts the preacher's heart into the preacher's sermon; prayer puts the preacher's sermon into the preacher's heart.

The heart makes the preacher. Men of great hearts are great preachers. Men of bad hearts may do a measure of good, but this is rare.

We have emphasized sermon-preparation until we have lost sight of the important thing to be prepared— the heart. A prepared heart is much better than a prepared sermon. A prepared heart will make a prepared sermon. Volumes have been written, laying down the mechanics and taste of sermon-making, until we have become possessed with the idea that this scaffolding is the building. The young preacher has been taught to lay out all his strength on the form, taste, beauty of his sermon as a mechanical and intellectual product. We have thereby cultivated a vicious taste among the people and raise the clamour for talent instead of grace, eloquence instead of piety, rhetoric instead of revelation, reputation and brilliancy instead of holiness. By it we have lost the true idea of preaching, lost preaching power, lost pungent conviction for sin,

lost the rich experience and elevated Christian character, lost the authority over consciences and lives which
always result from genuine preaching.

It would not do to say that preachers study too
much. Some of them do not study at all; others do not
study enough. Numbers do not study the right way
to show themselves workmen approved of God. But
our great lack is not in head culture, but in heart culture; not lack of knowledge, but lack of holiness is our
sad and telling defect—not that we know too much, but
that we do not meditate on God and His Word and
watch and fast and pray enough. The heart is the
great hindrance to our preaching. Words pregnant with
divine truth find in our hearts nonconductors; arrested,
they fall shorn and powerless.

Can ambition, that lusts after praise and place,
preach the gospel of Him who made himself of no
reputation and took on Him the form of a servant?
Can the proud, the vain, the egotistical, preach the
gospel of Him who was meek and lowly; can the bad-
tempered, passionate, selfish, hard, worldly man preach
the system which teems with long-suffering, self-denial,
tenderness, which imperatively demands separation
from enmity and crucifixion to the world?

The heart is the savior of the world. Heads do
not save. Genius, brains, brilliancy, strength, natural
gifts do not save. The gospel flows through hearts. All
the mightiest forces are heart forces. All the sweetest
and loveliest graces are heart graces. Great hearts
make great characters; great hearts make divine
characters. God is love. There is nothing great-

er than love, nothing greater than God. Hearts make heaven; heaven is love. There is nothing higher, nothing sweeter, than heaven. It is the heart and not the head which makes God's great preachers. The heart counts much every way in religion. The heart must speak from the pulpit. The heart must hear in the pew. In fact, we serve God with our hearts. Head homage does not pass current in heaven.

Unction is the art of preaching. The preacher who never had this unction never had the art of preaching. The preacher who has lost this unction has lost the art of preaching. Whatever other arts he may have and retain—the art of sermon-making, the art of eloquence, the art of great, clear thinking, the art of pleasing an audience—he has lost the divine art of preaching. This unction makes God's truth powerful and interesting, draws and attracts, edifies, convicts, saves. This unction vitalizes God's revealed truth, makes it living and life-giving. Even God's truth spoken without this unction is light, dead and deadening. Though abounding in truth, though weighty with thought, though sparkling with rhetoric, though pointed by logic, though powerful by earnestness, without this divine unction it issues in death and not life. Mr. Spurgeon says: "I wonder how long we might beat our brains before we could plainly put into words what is meant by preaching with unction. Yet he who preaches knows its presence and he who hears soon detects its absence. Samaria in famine typifies a discourse without it. Jerusalem, with her feast of fat things, full of marrow, may represent a sermon enriched with it. Everyone knows what the freshness of the morning is when Orient pearls abound on every blade of grass, but who can describe it, much less produce it of itself? Such is the mystery of spiritual anointing. We know, but we cannot tell to others what it is. It is as easy as it is foolish, to counterfeit it. Unction is a thing which you cannot manufacture, and its counterfeits are worse than worthless. Yet it is, in itself, priceless, and beyond measure needful if you would edify believers and bring sinners to Christ."

Unction is that indefinable, indescribable something which an old, renowned Scotch preacher described thus: "There is sometimes somewhat in preaching that cannot be described either to matter or to expression, and cannot be described what it is, or from whence it cometh, but with a sweet violence it pierces into the heart and affections and comes immediately from the Lord; but if there be any way to obtain such a thing, it is by the heavenly disposition of the speaker."

We call it unction. It is this unction which makes the Word of God "quick, and powerful, and sharper than any two-edged sword, piercing even to the dividing asunder of soul and spirit, and of the joints and marrow, and is a discerner of the thoughts and intents of the heart."

It is this unction which gives the words of the preacher such point, sharpness, and power, and which creates such friction and stir in many a dead congregation.

The same truths have been told in the strictness of the letter, smooth as human oil could make them; but no signs of life, not a pulse throb; all as peaceful as the grave and as dead. The same preacher in the meanwhile receives the baptism of this unction, the divine inflatus is upon him, the letter of the Word has been embellished and fired by this mysterious power, and the throbbings of life begin—life which receives or life which resists. The unction pervades and convicts the conscience and breaks the heart.

Unction is simply putting God in His own Word and on His own preacher. By mighty and great prayerfulness and by continual prayerfulness, it is all potential and personal to the preacher; it inspires and clarifies his intellect, gives insight and grasp and protecting power; it gives to the preacher heart-power, which is greater than head-power; and tenderness, purity, force, flow from the heart by it. Enlargement, freedom, fullness of thought, directness and simplicity of utterance are the fruits of this unction. Earnestness and unction look alike from some points of view. Earnestness may be readily and without detection substituted or mistaken for unction. It requires a spiritual eye and a spiritual taste to discriminate.

Earnestness may be sincere, serious, ardent, and persevering. It goes at a thing with good will, pursues it with perseverance, and urges it with ardor; puts force in it. But all these forces do not rise higher than the mere human. The man is in it—the whole man, with all that he has of will and heart, of brain and genius, of planning, working, and talking. He has set himself to some purpose which has mastered him, and he pursues to master it. There may be none of God in it. There may be little of God in it, because there is so much of the man in it.

It was said of a rather famous preacher of gifts, whose construction of Scripture was to his fancy or purpose, that he "grew very eloquent over his own exegesis." So men grow exceeding earnest over their own plans or movements. Earnestness may be selfishness simulated. What of unction? It is the indefinable in preaching which makes it preaching. It is that which distinguishes and separates preaching from all mere human addresses. It is the divine in preaching. It makes the preaching sharp to those who need sharpness. It distills as the dew to those who need to be refreshed. It is well described as

"... a two-edged sword
    Of heavenly temper keen,
And double were the wounds it made
    Where're it glanced between.
    'Twas death to sin; 'Twas life
    To all who mourned for sin.
It kindled and it silenced strife,
    Made war and peace within."

This unction comes to the preacher not in the study but in the closet. It is heaven's distillation in answer to prayer. It is the sweetest exhalation of the Holy Spirit. It impregnates, suffuses, softens, percolates, cuts, and soothes. It carries the Word like dynamite, like salt, like sugar; makes the Word a soother, and arraigner, a revealer, a searcher; makes the hearer a culprit or a saint, makes him weep like a child and live like a giant; opens his heart and his purse as gently, yet as strongly, as the spring opens the leaves. This unction is not the gift of genius. It is not found in the halls of learning. No eloquence can woo it. No industry can win it. No

prelatical hands can confer it. It is the gift of God—
the signet set to His own messengers. It is heaven's
knighthood given to the chosen, true, and brave ones
who have sought this anointed honor through many
an hour of tearful, wrestling prayer.

Earnestness is good and impressive; genius is gifted
and great. Thought kindles and inspires, but it takes a
more divine endowment, a more powerful energy than
earnestness or genius or thought to break the chains of
sin, to win the estranged and depraved hearts to God,
to repair the breaches and restore the Church to her
old ways of purity and power. Nothing but this holy
unction can do this.

In the Christian system unction is the anointing
of the Holy Ghost, separating unto God's work and
qualifying for it. This unction is the one divine enable-
ment by which the preacher accomplishes the peculiar
and saving ends of preaching. Without this unction
there are no true spiritual results accomplished; the
results and forces in preaching do not rise above the
results of unsanctified speech. Without unction the
former is as potent as the pulpit.

This divine unction on the preacher generates
through the Word of God the spiritual results that
flow from the gospel; and without this unction, these
results are not secured. Many pleasant impressions may
be made, but these all fall far below 'the ends of
gospel preaching. This unction may be simulated. There
are many things that look like it, there are many
results that resemble its effects; but they are foreign to
its results and to its nature. The fervor or softness ex-

cited by a pathetic or emotional sermon may look like
the movements of the divine unction, but they have no
pungent, penetrating, heart-breaking force. No heart-
healing balm is there in these surface, sympathetic,
emotional movements; they are not radical, neither
sin-searching nor sin-curing.

This divine unction is the one distinguishing feature
that separates true gospel preaching from all other
methods of presenting truth. It backs and interpene-
trates the revealed truth with all the force of God. It
illumines the Word and broadens and enriches the
intellect and empowers it to grasp and apprehend the
Word. It qualifies the preacher's heart, and brings it
to that condition of tenderness, of purity, of force and
light that are necessary to secure the highest results.
This unction gives to the preacher liberty and enlargement of thought and soul—a freedom, a fullness, and
directness of utterance that can be secured by no other
process.

This unction, the divine unction, this heavenly
anointing, is what the pulpit needs and must have.
This divine and heavenly oil put on by the imposition
of God's hand must soften and lubricate the whole
man—heart, head, spirit—until it separates him from
selfish motives and aims, separating him to everything
that is pure and God-like.

This unction is not an inalienable gift. It is a
conditional gift, and its presence is perpetuated and
increased by the same process by which it was first
secured; by unceasing prayer to God, by impassioned
desires after God, by estimating it, by seeking it with

tireless ardor, by deeming all else loss and failure without it.

How and whence comes this unction? Direct from God in answer to prayer. Praying hearts only are the hearts filled with this holy oil; praying lips only are anointed with this divine unction. *Prayer, much prayer, is the price of preaching unction; prayer, much prayer, is the one sole condition of keeping this unction.* Without unceasing prayer, the unction never comes to the preacher. Without perseverance in prayer, the unction, like the manna over-kept, breeds worms.

The apostles knew the necessity and worth of prayer to their ministry. They knew that their high commission as apostles, instead of relieving them from the necessity of prayer, committed them to it by a more urgent need, so that they were exceedingly jealous else some other important work should exhaust their time and prevent their praying as they ought; so they appointed laymen to look after the delicate and engrossing duties of ministering to the poor, that they (the apostles) might, unhindered, "give themselves continually to prayer and to the ministry of the word." Prayer is put first, and their relation to prayer is put most strongly—"give themselves to it," making a business of it, surrendering themselves to praying, putting fervor, urgency, perseverance, and time in it.

How holy, apostolic men devoted themselves to this divine work of prayer! "Night and day praying exceedingly," says Paul. "We will give ourselves continually to prayer" is the consensus of apostolic devotement. How these New Testament preachers laid themselves out in prayer for God's people! How they put God in force into their churches by their praying! These holy apostles did not vainly fancy that they had met their high and solemn duties by delivering faithfully God's Word, but their preaching was made to stick and tell by the ardor and insistence of their praying. Apostolic praying was as taxing, toilsome and imperative as apostolic preaching. They prayed mightily day and night to bring their people to the highest regions of faith and holiness.

Apostolic praying makes apostolic saints and keeps apostolic times of purity and power in the Church.

Preachers are pre-eminently God's leaders. They are primarily responsible for the condition of the Church. They shape its character, give tone and direction to its life.

Much every way depends on these leaders. They shape the times and the institutions. The Church is divine, the treasure it incases is heavenly, but it bears the imprint of the human. The treasure is in earthen vessels, and it smacks of the vessel. The Church of God makes, or is made by, its leaders. Whether it makes them or is made by them, it will be what its leaders are; spiritual if they are so, secular if they are, conglomerate if its leaders are. Israel's kings give character to Israel's piety. A church rarely revolts against or rises above the religion of its leaders. A prayerless ministry is the undertaker for all God's truth and for God's Church. Prayer, to the preacher, is not simply the duty of his profession, a privilege, but it is a necessity. Air is not more necessary to the lungs than prayer is to the preacher. It is absolutely necessary for the preacher to pray. It is an absolute necessity that the preacher be prayed for. These two propositions are wedded into a union which ought never to know any divorce: *the preacher must pray; the preacher must be prayed for.* It will take all the praying he can do, and all the praying he can get done, to meet the fearful responsibilities and gain the largest, truest success in his great work.

The more the preacher's eyes are opened to the nature, responsibility, and difficulties in his work, the more will he see, and if he be a true preacher, the more will he feel, the necessity of prayer; not only the increasing demand to pray himself, but to call on others to help him by their prayers.

Paul is an illustration of this. If any man could project the gospel by dint of personal force, by brain power, by culture, by personal grace, by God's apostolic commission, God's extraordinary call, that man was Paul. That the preacher must be a man given to prayer, Paul is an eminent example.

That the true apostolic preacher must have the prayers of other good people to give to his ministry its full quota of success, Paul is a pre-eminent example. He asks, he covets, he pleads in an impassioned way for the help of all God's saints. He knew that in the spiritual realm, as elsewhere, in union there is strength; that the concentration and aggregation of faith, desire, and prayer increased the volume of spiritual force until it became overwhelming and irresistible in its power. Units of prayer combined, like drops of water, make an ocean which defies resistance. So Paul, with his clear and full apprehension of spiritual dynamics, determined to make his ministry as impressive, as eternal, as irresistible, as the ocean, that by gathering all the scattered units of prayer and precipitating them on his ministry. Called, commissioned, chief of the apostles as he was, all his equipment was imperfect without the prayers of his people. He wrote letters everywhere, urging them to pray for him. Do you pray for your preacher? Do you pray for him in secret? Public prayers are of little worth unless they are founded on or followed up by private praying.

Our devotions are not measured by the clock, but time is of their essence. The ability to wait and stay and press belongs essentially to our intercourse with God. Hurry, everywhere unseeming and damaging, is so to an alarming extent in the great business of a communion with God. *Short devotions are the bane of deep piety*. Calmness, grasp, strength, are never the companions of hurry. Short devotions deplete spiritual vigor, arrest spiritual progress, sap spiritual foundations, blight the root and bloom of spiritual life. They are the prolific source of backsliding, the sure indication of a superficial piety; they deceive, blight, rot the seed, and impoverish the soil.

It is true that Bible prayers in word and print are short, but the praying men of the Bible were with God through many a sweet and holy wrestling hour. They won by few words but long waiting. The prayers Moses records may be short, but Moses prayed to God with fastings and mighty cryings forty days and nights.

The statement of Elijah's praying may be condensed to a few brief paragraphs, but doubtless Elijah, who, when "praying he prayed," spent many hours of fiery struggle and lofty intercourse with God before he could, with assured boldness, say to Ahab, "There shall not be dew nor rain these years, but according to my word." The verbal brief of Paul's prayers is short, but Paul "prayed night and day exceedingly." The *Lord's Prayer* is a divine epitome for infant lips, but the Man Christ Jesus prayed many an all-night ere His work was done; and His all-night and long-sustained devotions gave to His work its finish and perfection, and to His character the fullness and glory of its divinity.

Spiritual work is taxing work, and men are loath to do it. Praying, true praying, costs an outlay of serious attention and of time, which flesh and blood do not relish. Few persons are made of such strong fiber that they will make a costly outlay when surface work will pass as well in the market. To be little with God is to be little for God. To cut short the praying makes the whole religious character short, skrimp, niggardly, and slovenly. William Wilberforce, the peer of kings, said: "I must secure more time for private devotions. I have been living far too public for me. The shortening of private devotions starves the soul; it grows lean and faint. I have been keeping too late hours."

We must learn anew the worth of prayer, enter anew the school of prayer. There is nothing which it takes more time to learn. And if we would learn the wondrous art, we must not give a fragment here and there, "a little talk with Jesus," as the tiny saintlets

sing—but we must demand and hold with iron grasp
the best hours of the day for God and prayer, or there
will be no praying worth the name. Who prays as
Jacob prayed—till he is crowned as a prevailing, princely intercessor? Who prays as Elijah prayed—till all the
locked-up forces of nature were unsealed and the fam-
ine-stricken land bloomed as the garden of God?

Who prayed as Jesus Christ prayed—as out upon
the mountain He "continued all night in prayer to
God"? The apostles "gave themselves to prayer"—the
most difficult thing to get a man or even the preachers
to do. Laymen there are who will give their money—
some of them in rich abundance—but they will not
"give themselves" to prayer, without which their money
is but a curse. There are plenty of preachers who will
deliver great and eloquent addresses on the need of
revival and the spread of the kingdom of God, but
not many there are who will do that without which
all preaching and organizing are worse than vain—
pray. It is out of date, almost a lost art, and *the greatest benefactor this age could have is a man who will
bring the preachers and the Church back to prayer.*

The Necessity
Of Prayer

My creed leads me to think that prayer is efficacious, and surely a day's asking God to overrule all events is not lost. Still there is a great feeling that when a man is praying he is doing nothing, and this feeling makes us give undue importance to work, sometimes even to the hurrying over or even to the neglect of prayer.

Do not we rest in our day too much on the arm of flesh? Cannot the same wonders be done now as of old? Do not the eyes of the Lord run to and fro throughout the whole earth still to shew himself strong on behalf of those who put their trust in Him? Oh! that God would give me more practical faith in Him! Where is now the Lord God of Elijah? HE IS WAITING FOR ELIJAH TO CALL ON HIM!

CHAPTER FOUR

THE NECESSITY OF PRAYER

In any study of the principles, and the procedure of prayer, of its activities and enterprises, the first place, must of necessity, be given to faith. It is the initial quality in the heart of any man who essays to talk to the Unseen. He must, out of sheer helplessness, stretch forth hands of faith. He *must* believe, where he cannot prove. In the ultimate issue, prayer is simply faith, claiming its natural yet marvelous prerogatives—faith taking possession of its illimitable inheritance.

True godliness is just as true, steady, and persevering in the realm of faith as it is in the province of prayer. Moreover, when faith ceases to pray, it ceases to live.

Faith does the impossible because it brings God to undertake for us, and nothing is impossible with God. How great—without qualification nor limitation—is the power of faith! If doubt be banished from the heart, and unbelief made stranger there, what we ask of God shall surely come to pass, and a believer hath vouchsafed to Him, "whatsoever he saith."

Prayer projects faith on God, and God on the world. Only God can move mountains, but faith and prayer move God. Obedience helps faith, and faith, in turn, helps obedience. To do God's will is essential to true faith, and faith is necessary to implicit obedience.

Yet faith is called upon, and that right often, to wait in patience before God, and is prepared for God's seeming delays in answering prayer. Faith does not grow disheartened because prayer is not immediately honored; it takes God at His Word and lets Him take what time He chooses in fulfilling His purposes, and in carrying on His work. There is bound to be much delay and long days of waiting for true faith, but faith accepts the conditions—knows there will be delays in answering prayer, and regards such delays as times of testing, in the which it is privileged to show its mettle and the stern stuff of which it is made.

As every day demands its bread, so every day demands its prayer. No amount of praying done today will suffice for tomorrow's praying. On the other hand, no praying for tomorrow is of any great value to us today. Today's manna is what we need; tomorrow God will see that our needs are supplied. This is the faith which God seeks to inspire. So leave tomorrow, with its cares, its needs, its troubles, in God's hands. There is no storing of tomorrow's grace or tomorrow's praying; neither is there any laying up of today's grace to meet tomorrow's necessities. We cannot have tomorrow's grace, we cannot eat tomorrow's bread, we cannot do tomorrow's praying. "Sufficient unto the day is the evil thereof"; and, most assuredly, if we possess faith, sufficient also, will be the good.

Genuine, authentic faith must be definite and free of doubt. Not simply general in character; not a mere belief in the being, goodness and power of God, but a faith which believes in the things which "he saith, shall come to pass." As the faith is specific, so the answer likewise will be definite: "He shall have whatsoever he saith." Faith and prayer select the things, and God commits himself to do the very things which faith and persevering faith nominate, and petition Him to accomplish.

Our chief concern is with our faith—the problems of its growth, and the activities of its vigorous maturity. A faith which grasps and holds in its keeping the very thing it asks for, without wavering, doubt or fear—that is the faith we need—faith, such as is a pearl of great price, in the process and practice of prayer. Faith must be definite, specific; an unqualified, unmistakable request for the things asked for. It is not to be a vague, indefinite, shadowy thing; it must be something more than an abstract belief in God's willingness and ability to do for us. It is to be a definite, specific asking for, and expecting the things for which we ask. Note the reading of Mark 11:23: "And shall *not doubt* in his heart, but *shall believe* that those things which he saith shall come to pass; he shall have whatsoever he saith." Faith is not an abstract belief in the Word of God, nor a mere mental credence, nor a simple assent of the understanding and will; nor is it a passive acceptance of facts, however sacred or thorough. Faith is an operation of God, a divine illumination, a holy energy implanted by the Word of God and the Spirit in the human soul—a spiritual, divine prin-

ciple which takes of the supernatural and makes it a
thing apprehendable by the faculties of time and sense.

Faith deals with God, and is conscious of God.
It deals with the Lord Jesus Christ and sees in Him a
Saviour; it deals with God's Word, and lays hold of
the truth; it deals with the Spirit of God, and is
energized and inspired by its holy fire. God is a
great objective of faith; for faith rests its whole weight
on His Word. Faith is not an aimless act of the soul,
but a looking to God and resting upon His promises.
Just as love and hope have always an objective, so
also has faith. Faith is not believing just *anything*; it
is believing God, resting in Him, trusting His Word.

Faith gives birth to prayer, and grows stronger,
strikes deeper, rises higher, in the struggles and wrestlings of mighty petitioning. Faith is the substance of
things hoped for, the assurance and realization of the
inheritance of the saints. Faith, too, is humble and
persevering. It can wait and pray; it can stay on its
knees, or lie in the dust. It is the one great condition
of prayer; the lack of it lies at the root of all poor
praying, feeble praying, little praying, unanswered
praying. What an era of glorious achievements would
dawn for the Church and for the world, if only there
could be reproduced a race of saints of like mighty
faith, of like wonderful praying as those found in
Hebrews 11. It is not the intellectually great that
the Church needs; nor is it men of wealth that the
times demand. It is not people of great social influence
that this day requires. Above everybody and everything
else, it is men of faith, men of mighty prayer, men
and women after the fashion of the saints and heroes

enumerated in Hebrews, who "obtained a good report through faith," that the Church and the whole wide world of humanity needs.

Many men, of this day, obtain a good report because of their money-giving, their great mental gifts and talents, but few there be who obtain a "good report" because of their great faith in God, or because of the wonderful things which are being wrought through their great praying. Today, as much as at any time, we need men of great faith and men who are great in prayer. Doubt and fears are the twin foes of faith. Sometimes they actually usurp the place of faith, and although we pray, it is a restless, disquieted prayer that we offer, uneasy and often complaining. Peter failed to walk on Gennesaret because he permitted the waves to break over him and swamp the power of his faith. Taking his eyes from the Lord and regarding the water all about him, he began to sink and had to cry for succour—"Lord, save, or I perish!"

All of us need to mark well and heed the caution given in Hebrews: "Take heed, brethren, lest there be in any of you an evil heart of unbelief, in departing from the living God."

We need, also, to guard against unbelief as we would against an enemy. Faith needs to be cultivated. We need to keep on praying, "Lord, increase our faith," for faith is susceptible of increase. Paul's tribute to the Thessalonians was that their faith grew exceedingly. Faith is increased by exercise, by being put to use. It is nourished by sore trials. Faith grows by reading and meditating upon the Word of God. Most, and best of all, faith thrives in an atmosphere of prayer.

It would be well, if all of us were to stop and inquire personally of ourselves: "Have I faith in God? Have I *real* faith—faith which keeps me in perfect peace about the things of earth and the things of heaven?" This is the most important question a man can propound and expect to be answered. And there is another question, closely akin to it in significance and importance—"Do I really pray to God so that He really hears me and answers my prayers? And do I truly pray unto God so that I get direct from Him the things I ask of Him?"

It was claimed for Augustus Cæsar that he found Rome a city of wood, and left it a city of marble. The pastor who succeeds in changing his people from a prayerless to a prayerful people, has done a greater work than did Augustus in changing a city from wood to marble. And after all, this is the prime work of the preacher. The preacher is not sent to merely induce men to join the church, nor merely to get them to do better. It is to get them to pray, to trust God, and to keep God ever before their eyes, that they may not sin against Him.

By faith are we saved, and by faith we *stay* saved. Prayer induces us to a life of faith. Paul declared that the life he lived, he lived by faith in the Son of God, who loved him and gave Himself for him, that he walked by faith and not by sight.

Faith makes prayer effectual, and in a certain important sense, must precede it. "For he that cometh to God must believe that he is, and that he is a rewarder of them that diligently seek him."

Before prayer ever starts toward God, before its petition is preferred, before its requests are made known—faith must have gone on ahead; must have asserted its belief in the existence of God; must have given its assent to the gracious truth that "God is a rewarder of those that diligently seek his face." This is the primary step in praying. In this regard, while faith does not bring the blessing, yet it puts prayer in a position to ask for it, and leads to another step toward realization, by aiding the petitioner to believe that God is able and willing to bless.

Faith starts prayer to work—clears the way to the mercy-seat. It gives assurance, first of all, that there is a mercy-seat, and that there the High Priest awaits the pray-ers and the prayers. Faith opens the way for prayer to approach God. But it does more. It accompanies prayer at every step she takes. It is her inseparable companion and when requests are made unto God, it is faith which turns the asking into obtaining. And faith follows prayer, since the spiritual life into which the believer is led by prayer is a life of faith. The one prominent characteristic of the experience into which believers are brought through prayer is not a life of works, but of faith.

All questioning must be watched against and eschewed. Fear and peradventure have no place in true praying. Faith must assert itself and bid these foes to prayer depart.

The spirit of a pilgrim greatly facilitates praying. An earth-bound, earth-satisfied spirit cannot pray. In such a heart, the flame of spiritual desire has either gone out or is smouldering in faintest glow. The wings of its faith are clipped, its eyes are filmed, its tongue silenced. But they, who in unswerving faith and unceasing prayer wait continually upon the Lord, *do* renew their strength, *do* mount up with wings as eagles, *do* run and are not weary, *do* walk and are not faint.

Prayer does not stand alone. It is not an isolated duty and independent principle. It lives in association with other Christian duties, is wedded to other principles, is a partner with other graces. But to faith, prayer is indissolubly joined. Faith gives it color and tone, shapes its character, and secures its results.

Trust is faith become absolute, ratified, consummated. There is, when all is said and done, a sort of venture in faith and its exercise. But trust is *firm belief*, it is faith in full flower. Trust is a conscious act, a fact of which we are sensible.

Trust, like life, is feeling, though much more than feeling. An unfelt life is a contradiction; an unfelt trust is a misnomer, a delusion, a contradiction. Trust is the most felt of all attributes. It is *all* feeling, and it works only by love. An unfelt love is as impossible as an unfelt trust. The trust of which we are now speaking is a conviction. An unfelt conviction? How absurd!

Trust sees God doing things here and now. Yea, more. It rises to a lofty eminence, and looking into the invisible and the eternal realizes that God has done things, and regards them as being already done. Trust brings eternity into the annals and happenings of time, transmutes the substance of hope into the reality of fruition, and changes promise into present possession. We know when we trust just as we know when we see, just as we are conscious of our sense of touch. Trust sees, receives, holds. Trust is its own witness. Yet, quite often, faith is too weak to obtain God's greatest good, immediately; so it has to wait in loving, strong, prayerful, pressing obedience, until it grows in strength, and is able to bring down the eternal into the realms of experience and time. To this point, trust masses all its forces. Here it holds. And in the struggle, trust's grasp becomes mightier and grasps for itself all that God has done for it in His eternal wisdom and plentitude of grace.

In the matter of waiting in prayer, mightiest prayer, faith rises to its highest plain and becomes indeed the gift of God. It becomes the blessed disposition and expression of the soul which is secured by a constant intercourse with, an unwearied application to God. Trust, in a historical fact or in a mere record may be a very passive thing, but trust in the person vitalizes the quality, fructifies it, informs it with love. The trust which informs prayer centers in a Person.

Our Lord puts trust as the very foundation of praying. The background of prayer is trust. The whole issuance of Christ's ministry and work was dependent upon implicit trust in His Father. The center of trust is God. Mountains of difficulties, and all other hindrances to prayer are moved out of the way by trust and his virile henchman, faith. When trust is perfect and without doubt, prayer is simply the out-stretched hand, ready to receive. Trust perfected is prayer perfected.

Trust looks to receive the thing asked for—and gets it. Trust is not a belief that God *can* bless, that He *will* bless, but that He *does* bless, here and now. Trust always operates in the present tense. Hope looks forward to the future. Trust looks to the present. Hope expects. Trust possesses. Trust receives what prayer acquires. So that what prayer needs, at all times, is abiding and abundant trust.

Desire is not merely a simple wish; it is a deep-seated craving; an intense longing for attainment. In the realm of spiritual affairs, it is an important adjunct to prayer. So important is it, that one might say, almost, that desire is an absolute essential of prayer. Desire precedes prayer, accompanies it, is followed by it. Desire goes before prayer, and by it, is created and intensified. Prayer is the oral expression of desire. If prayer is asking God for something, then prayer must be expressed. Prayer comes out into the open. Desire is silent. Prayer is heard; desire, unheard. The deeper the desire, the stronger the prayer. Without desire, prayer is a meaningless mumble of words. Such perfunctory, formal praying, with no heart, no feeling, no real desire accompanying it, is to be shunned like a pestilence. Its exercise is a waste of precious time, and from it, no real blessing accrues.

In prayer, we are shut up to the name, merit, and intercessory virtue of Jesus Christ, our great High Priest. Probing down below the accompanying conditions and forces in prayer, we come to its vital basis which is sealed in the human heart. It is not simply our need; it is the heart's yearning for what we need, and for which we feel impelled to pray. Desire is the will in action; a strong, conscious longing, excited in the inner nature for some great good. Desire exalts the object of its longing, and fixes the mind on it. It has choice, and fixedness, and flame in it; and prayer, based thereon, is explicit and specific. It knows its need, feels and sees the thing that will meet it, and hastens to acquire it.

The dampening of the flame of holy desire is destructive of the vital and aggressive forces in church life. God requires to be represented by a fiery Church, or He is not in any proper sense, represented at all. God, himself, is all on fire, and His Church, if it is to be like Him, must also be at white heat. The great and eternal interests of heaven-born, God-given religion are the only things about which His Church can afford to be on fire. Yet holy zeal need not to be fussy in order to be consuming. Our Lord was the incarnate antithesis of nervous excitability, the absolute opposite of intolerant or clamorous declamation, yet the zeal of God's house consumed Him; and the world is still feeling the glow of His fierce, consuming flame and responding to it with an ever-increasing readiness and an ever-enlarging response.

"I would thou wert cold or hot. So then because thou art lukewarm, and neither cold or hot, I will spue thee out of my mouth."

This was God's expressed judgment on the lack of fire in one of the seven churches, and it is His indictment against individual Christians for the fatal want of sacred zeal. In prayer, fire is the motive power. Religious principles which do not emerge in flame have neither force nor effect. Flame is the wing on which faith ascends; fervency is the soul of prayer. It was the "effectual, fervent prayer" which availed much. Love is kindled in the flame, and ardency is its life. Flame is the air which true Christian experience breathes. It feeds on fire; it can withstand anything, rather than a feeble flame; and it dies chilled and starved to its vitals when the surrounding atmosphere is frigid or lukewarm.

True prayer *must* be aflame. Christian life and character need to be all on fire. Lack of spiritual heat creates more infidelity than lack of faith. Nothing short of being red hot for God can keep the glow of heaven in our hearts, these chilly days. The early Methodists had no heating apparatus in their churches. And they declared that the *flame in the pew* and the *fire in the pulpit* must suffice to keep them warm.

This flame is not mental vehemence nor fleshly energy. It is divine fire in the soul, intense, dross-consuming—the very essence of the Spirit of God. No erudition, no purity of diction, no width of mental outlook, no flowers of eloquence, no grace of person, can atone for lack of fire. Prayer ascends by fire. Flame gives prayer access as well as wings, acceptance as well as energy. There is no incense without fire; no prayer without flame.

Ardent desire is the basis of unceasing prayer. It is not a shallow, fickle inclination, but a strong yearning, an unquenchable ardor, which impregnates, glows, burns, and fixes the heart. It is the flame of a present and active principle mounting up to God. It is ardor-propelled by desire, that burns its way to the Throne of mercy, and gains its plea. It is the pertinacity of desire that gives triumph to the conflict in a great struggle of prayer. It is the burden of a weighty desire that sobers, makes restless, and reduces to quietness the soul just emerged from its mighty wrestlings. It is the embracing character of desire which arms prayer with a thousand pleas, and robes it with an invincible courage and an all-conquering power.

Without desire, there is no burden of soul, no sense of need, no ardency, no vision, no strength, no glow of faith. There is no mighty pressure, no holding on to God with a deathless, despairing grasp—"I will not let thee go, except thou bless me." There is no utter self-abandonment, as there was with Moses, when, lost in the throes of a desperate, pertinacious, and all-consuming plea, he cried, "Yet now, if thou wilt forgive their sin—and if not, blot me, I pray thee, out of thy book." Or, as there was with John Knox when he pleaded: "Give me Scotland, or I die!"

God draws mightily near to the praying soul. To see God, to know God, and to live for God—these form the objective of all true praying. Thus, praying is, after all, inspired to seek after God. Prayer-desire is inflamed to see God, to have clearer, fuller, sweeter, and richer revelation of God. So to those who thus pray, the

Bible becomes a *new* Bible, and Christ a new Saviour,
by the light and revelation of the inner chamber.

Fervorless prayer has no heart in it; it is an empty
thing, an unfit vessel. Heart, soul, and life must try
and place all real praying. Heaven must be made to
feel the force of this crying unto God. Prayers must
be red hot. It is the fervent prayer that is effectual
and that availeth. Coldness of spirit hinders praying;
prayer cannot live in a wintery atmosphere. Chilly
surroundings freeze out petitioning, and dry up the
springs of supplication. It takes fire to make prayers
go. Warmth of soul creates an atmosphere favorable
to prayer because it is favorable to fervency. By flame,
prayer ascends to heaven. Yet fire is not fuss nor
heat, nor noise. Heat is intensity—something that
glows and burns. Heaven is a mighty poor market for
ice.

The wrestling quality of importunate prayer does
not spring from physical vehemence or fleshly energy.
It is not an impulse of energy, not a mere earnestness
of soul; it is an inwrought force, a faculty implanted
and aroused by the Holy Spirit. Virtually it is the
intercession of the Spirit of God in us; it is, moreover, "the effectual, fervent prayer . . . [which] availeth
much." The Divine Spirit informing every element
within us, with the energy of His own striving, is the
essence of the importunity which urges our praying
at the mercy-seat, to continue until the fire falls and
the blessing descends. This wrestling in prayer may not
be boisterous nor vehement, but quiet, tenacious and
urgent. Silent it may be, when there are no visible
outlets for its mighty forces.

Nothing distinguishes the children of God so clearly and strongly as prayer. It is the one infallible mark and test of being a Christian. Christian people are prayerful; the worldly-minded, prayerless. Christians call on God; worldlings ignore God, and call not on His name. But even the Christian has need to cultivate *continual* prayer. Prayer must be habitual, but much more than a habit. It is duty, but one that rises far above and goes beyond the ordinary implications of the term. It is the expression of a relation to God, a yearning for divine communion. It is the outward and upward flow of the inward life toward its original fountain. It is an assertion of the soul's paternity, a claiming of the sonship which links man to the Eternal. He prays not at all who does not press his plea. Cold prayers have no claim on heaven, and no hearing in the courts above. Fire is the life of prayer, and heaven is reached by flaming importunity arising in an ascending scale.

Importunate praying never faints nor grows weary; it is never discouraged; it never yields to cowardice, but is buoyed up and sustained by a hope that knows no despair, and a faith which will not let go.

Importunate praying has patience to wait and strength to continue. It never prepares itself to quit praying, and declines to rise from its knees till an answer is received.

"Prayer governs conduct and conduct makes character. Conduct is what we do; character is what we are. Conduct is the outward life. Character is the life unseen, hidden within, yet evidenced by that which is seen. Conduct is external, seen from without; character is internal—operating within. In the economy of grace, conduct is the offspring of character. Character is the state of heart, conduct is outward expression. Character is the root of the tree, conduct, the fruit it bears.

The office of prayer is to change the character and conduct of men, and in countless instances, has been wrought by prayer. At this point, prayer, by its credentials, has proved its divinity. And just as it is the office of prayer to effect this, so it is the prime work of the Church to take hold of evil men and make them good. Its mission is to change human nature, to change character, influence behavior, to revolutionize conduct.

A product reflects and partakes of the character of the manufactury which makes it. A righteous church with a righteous purpose makes righteous men.

Prayer produces cleanliness of heart and purity of life. It can produce nothing else. Unrighteous conduct is born of prayerlessness; the two go hand in hand. *Prayer and sinning cannot keep company with each other*. One or the other must, of necessity, stop. Get men to pray, and they will quit sinning, because prayer creates a distaste for sinning, and so works upon the heart that evil-doing becomes repugnant, and the entire nature lifted to a reverent contemplation of high and holy things.

Prayer is based on character. What we are with God gauges our influence with Him. It was the inner character, not the outward seeming, of such men as Abraham, Job, David, Moses, and all others, who had such influence with God in the days of old. And, today, it is not so much our words as what we really are, which weighs with God. Conduct affects character, of course, and counts for much in our praying. At the same time, character affects conduct to a far greater extent, and has a superior influence over prayer. Our life not only gives color to our praying, but body as well. But bad living means bad praying, and in the end, no praying at all. *We pray feebly because we live feebly*. The stream of prayer cannot rise righer than the fountain of living. The force of the inner chamber is made up of the energy which flows from the confluent streams of living. And the weakness of living grows out of shallowness and shoddiness of character.

Quite often, Christian experience founders on the rock of conduct. Beautiful theories are marred by ugly lives. The most difficult thing about piety, as it is the most impressive. is to be able to live it. *It is the life which counts*, and our praying suffers, as do other phases of our religious experience, from bad living.

Praying which does not result in right thinking and right living is a farce. We have missed the whole office of prayer if it fails to purge character and rectify conduct. We have failed entirely to apprehend the virtue of prayer, if it brings not about the revolutionizing of the life. In the very nature of things, we must quit praying or else we must quit our bad conduct.

Cold, formal praying may exist side by side with

bad conduct, but such praying, in the estimation of God, is no praying at all. Our praying advances in power, just in so far as it rectifies the life. Growing in purity and devotion to God will be a more prayerful life.

The character of the inner life is a condition of effectual praying. As is the life, so will the praying be. An inconsistent life obstructs praying and neutralizes what little praying we may do. Always, it is "the prayer of the righteous man which availeth much." Indeed, one may go further and assert that it is only the prayer of the righteous which avails anything at all—at any time. Praying sets him who prays to the great business of "working out his salvation with fear and trembling"; puts him to watching his temper, conversation and conduct; causes him to "walk circumspectly, redeeming the time"; enables him to "walk worthy of the vocation wherewith he is called, with all lowliness and meekness"; gives him a high incentive to pursue his pilgrimage consistently by "shunning every evil way, and walking in the good."

What is obedience? It is doing God's will; it is keeping His commandments. How many of the commandments constitutes obedience? To keep half of them, and to break the other half—is that real obedience? To keep all the commandments but one—is that obedience? On this point James the apostle is most explicit: "Whosoever shall keep the whole law," he declares, "and yet offend in one point, he is guilty of all."

Does God give commandments which men cannot obey? Is He so arbitrary, so severe, so unloving, as to issue commandments which cannot be obeyed? The answer is that in all the annals of Holy Scripture, not a single instance is recorded of God having commanded any man to do anything which was beyond his power. Is God so unjust and so inconsiderate as to require of man that which he is unable to render? Surely not. To infer it is to slander the character of God.

Let us ponder this thought a moment: Do earthly parents require of their children duties which they cannot perform? Where is the father who would think, even of being so unjust and so tyrannical? Is God less kind and just than faulty, earthly parents? Are they better and more just than a perfect God? How utterly foolish and untenable a thought!

Obedience is love, fulfilling every command, love expressing itself. Obedience, therefore, is not a hard demand made upon us any more than is the service a husband renders his wife, or a wife renders her husband. Love delights to obey and please whom it loves. There are no hardships in love. There may be exactions, but no irk. There are no impossible tasks for love.

If any should complain that humanity, under the Fall, is too weak and helpless to obey these high commands of God, the reply is in order that, through the Atonement of Christ, man is enabled to obey. The Atonement is God's Enabling Act. That which God works in us, in regeneration and through the agency of the Holy Spirit, bestows enabling grace sufficient for all that is required of us, under the Atonement.

This grace is furnished without measure, in answer to prayer. So that, while God commands, He, at the same time, stands pledged to give us all necessary strength of will in grace or soul to meet His demands. This being true, man is without excuse for his disobedience and eminently censurable for refusing or failing to secure requisite grace, whereby he may serve the Lord with reverence, and with godly fear. There is one important consideration those who declare it to be impossible to keep God's commandments strangely overlook, and that is the vital truth which declares that through prayer and faith, man's nature is changed, and made partaker of the divine nature; that there is taken out of him all reluctance to obey God, and that his natural inability to keep God's commandments, growing out of his fallen and helpless state, is gloriously removed. By this radical change which is wrought in his moral nature, a man receives power to obey God in every way and to yield full and glad allegiance. Then he can say, "I delight to do thy will, oh my God." Not only is the rebellion incident to the natural man removed, but a heart which gladly obeys God's Word is blessedly received.

The Essentials
Of Prayer

Bear up the hands that hang down, by faith and prayer; support the tottering knees. Have you any days of fasting and prayer? Storm the throne of grace and persevere therein, and mercy will come down.

—John Wesley

"Nothing is impossible to industry," said one of the seven sages of Greece. Let us change the word industry for persevering prayer, and the motto will be more Christian and more worthy of universal adoption.

I am persuaded that we are all more deficient in a spirit of prayer than in any other grace. God loves importunate prayer so much that He will not give us much blessing without it. And the reason that He loves such prayer is that He loves us and knows that it is a necessary preparation for our receiving the richest blessings which He is waiting and longing to bestow. I never prayed sincerely and earnestly for anything but it came at some time—no matter how distant a day, somehow in some shape, probably the last I would have devised, it came.

—Adoniram Judson

CHAPTER FIVE

THE ESSENTIALS OF PRAYER

Holiness is wholeness, and so God wants holy men, men whole-hearted and true, for His service and for the work of praying. "And the very God of peace sanctify you wholly; and I pray God your whole spirit and soul and body be preserved blameless unto the coming of our Lord Jesus Christ." These are the sort of men God wants for leaders of the hosts of Israel, and these are the kind out of which the praying class is formed.

Man is a trinity in one, and yet man is neither a trinity nor a dual creature when he prays, but a unit. Man is one in all the essentials and acts and attitudes of piety. Soul, spirit, and body are to unite in all things pertaining to life and godliness. The body, first of all, engages in prayer, since it assumes the praying attitude in prayer. Prostration of the body becomes us in praying as well as prostration of the soul. The attitude of the body counts much in prayer, although it is true that the heart may be haughty and lifted up, and the mind listless and wandering, and the praying a mere form, even while the knees are bent in prayer.

Daniel kneeled upon his knees three times a day in prayer. Solomon kneeled in prayer at the dedication of the temple. Our Lord in Gethsemane prostrated himself in that memorable season of praying just before His betrayal. Where there is earnest and faithful praying the body always takes on the form most suited to the state of the soul at the time. The body, that far, joins the soul in praying. The entire man must pray. The whole man—life, heart, temper, mind—is in it. Each and all join in the prayer exercise.

Clear mental action, right thinking, an enlightened understanding, and faith reasoning powers, come from praying. Divine guidance means God so moving and impressing the mind, that we shall make wise and safe decisions. "The meek will he guide in judgment." Many a praying preacher has been greatly helped just at this point. The unction of the Holy One which comes upon the preacher invigorates the mind, loosens up thought and gives utterance. This is the explanation of former days when men of very limited education had such wonderful liberty of the Spirit in praying and preaching. Their thoughts flowed as a stream of water. Their entire intellectual machinery felt the impulse of the Divine Spirit's gracious influences.

To be humble is to have a low estimate of one's self. It is to be modest, lowly, with a disposition to seek obscurity. Humility retires itself from the public gaze. It does not seek publicity nor hunt for high places, neither does it care for prominence. Humility is retiring in its nature. Self-abasement belongs to humility. It is given to self-depreciation. It never exalts itself in the eyes of others nor even in the eyes of itself. Modesty is one of its most prominent characteristics. In humility there is a total absence of pride, and it is at the very farthest distance from anything like self-conceit.

There is no self-praise in humility. Rather it has the disposition to praise others. "In honor preferring one another." It is not given to self-exaltation. Humility does not love the uppermost seats and aspire to the high places. It is willing to take the lowest seat and prefers those places where it will be unnoticed. The prayer of humility is after this fashion:

> "Never let the world break in,
> Fix a mighty gulf between;
> Keep me humble and unknown,
> Prized and loved by Thee alone."

God puts a great price on humility of heart. It is good to be clothed with humility as with a garment. It is written, "God resisteth the proud, but giveth grace to the humble." That which brings the praying soul near to God is humility of heart. That which gives wings to prayer is lowliness of mind. That which gives ready access to the throne of grace is self-depreciation. Pride, self-esteem, and self-praise effectually shut the door of prayer. He who would come to God must approach Him with self hidden from his eyes. He must not be puffed up with self-conceit, nor be possessed with an over-estimate of his virtues and good works.

Humility is a rare Christian grace, of great price in the courts of heaven, entering into and being an inseparable condition of effectual praying.

Our prayers must be set low before they can ever rise high. Our prayers must have much of the dust on them before they can ever have much of the glory of the skies in them.

Humility is an indispensable requisite of true prayer. It must be an attribute, a characteristic of prayer. Humility must be in the praying character as light is in the sun. Prayer has no beginning, no ending, no being, without humility. As a ship is made for the sea, so prayer is made for humility, and so humility is made for prayer.

Humility is not abstraction from self, nor does it ignore thought about self. It is a many-phased principle. Humility is born by looking at God, and His holiness, and then looking at self and man's unholiness. Humility loves obscurity and silence, dreads applause, esteems the virtues of others, excuses their faults with mildness, easily pardons injuries, fears contempt less and less, and sees baseness and falsehood in pride. A true nobleness and greatness are in humility.

Humility holds in its keeping the very life of prayer. Neither pride nor vanity can pray. Humility, though, is much more than the absence of vanity and pride. It is a positive quality, a substantial fort, which energizes prayer. There is no power in prayer to ascend without it. Humility springs from a lowly estimate of ourselves and of our deservings.

Humility is the first and last attribute of Christly religion, and the first and last attribute of Christly praying. There is no Christ without humility. There is no praying without humility. If thou would'st learn well the art of praying, then learn well the lesson of humility.

Devotion belongs to the inner life and lives in the closet, but also appears in the public services of the sanctuary. It is part of the very spirit of true worship, and is of the nature of the spirit of prayer. Devotion belongs to the devout man whose thoughts and feelings are devoted to God. Such a man has a mind given up wholly to religion, and possesses a strong affection for God and an ardent love for His house. Cornelius was "a devout man, one that feared God with all his house, which gave much alms to the people and prayed always." "Devout men carried Stephen to his burial." "One Ananias, a devout man, according to the law," was sent unto Saul when he was blind, to tell him what the Lord would have him do. God can wonderfully use such men, for devout men are His chosen agents in carrying forward His plans.

Prayer thrives in the atmosphere of true devotion. It is easy to pray when in the spirit of devotion. The attitude of mind and the state of heart implied in devotion make prayer effectual in reaching the throne of grace. God dwells where the spirit of devotion resides. All the graces of the Spirit are nourished and grow well in the environment created by devotion.

This is a busy age, bustling and active, and this bustling spirit has invaded the church of God. Its religious performances are many. The church works at religion with the order, precision and force of real

machinery. But too often it works with the heartless-
ness of the machine. There is much of the treadmill
movement in our ceaseless round and routine of religious doings. We pray without praying. We sing without singing with the spirit and the understanding.
We have music without the praise of God in it or
near it. We go to church by habit, and come home all
too gladly when the benediction is pronounced. We
read our accustomed chapter in the Bible, and feel
quite relieved when the task is done. We say our
prayers by rote, as a school boy recites his lesson,
and are not sorry when the amen is uttered.

The spirit of devotion is not merely the aroma of
religion, but the stalk and stem on which religion
grows. It is the salt which penetrates and makes
savory all religious acts. It is the sugar which sweetens
duty, self-denial and sacrifice. It is the bright coloring
which relieves the dullness of religious performances.
It dispels frivolity and drives away all skin-deep forms
of worship, and makes worship a serious and deep-
seated service, impregnating body, soul and spirit with
its heavenly infusion.

The spirit of devotion pervades the saints in heaven
and characterizes the worship of heaven's angelic in-
telligences. No devotionless creatures are in that heavenly world. God is there, and His very presence begets
the spirit of reverence, of awe, and of filial fear. If we
would be partakers with them after death, we must first
learn the spirit of devotion on earth before we get
there.

To be too busy with God's work to commune with

God, to be busy doing church work without taking time to talk to God about His work, is the highway to backsliding, and many people have walked therein to the hurt of their immortal souls.

Thanksgiving is just what the word itself signifies— the giving of thanks to God. It is giving something to God in words which we feel at heart for blessings received. Gratitude arises from the contemplation of the goodness of God. It is bred by serious meditation on what God has done for us. Both gratitude and thanksgiving point to, and have to do with, God and His mercies. The heart is consciously grateful to God. The soul gives expression to that heart-felt gratitude to God in words or acts. Praise is so distinctly and definitely wedded to prayer, so inseparably joined, that they cannot be divorced. Praise is dependent on prayer for its full volume and its sweetest melody.

Giving thanks is the very life of prayer. It is its fragrance and music, its poetry and its crown. Prayer is bringing the desired down so it breaks out into praise and thanksgiving.

The Weapon
Of Prayer

That was a grand action by Jerome, one of the Roman fathers. He laid aside all pressing engagements and went to fulfill the call God gave him, viz., to translate the Holy Scriptures. His congregations were larger than many preachers' of today, but he said to his people, "Now it is necessary that the Scriptures be translated; you must find you another minister. I am bound for the wilderness and shall not return until my task is finished." Away he went and labored and prayed until he produced the Latin Vulgate which will last as long as the world stands. So we must say to our friends, "I must away and have time for prayer and solitude." And though we did not write Latin Vulgates, yet our work will be immortal: Glory to God.

—Charles Haddon Spurgeon

Lord Jesus, cause me to know in my daily experience the glory and sweetness of Thy Name, then teach me how to use it in my prayer, so that I may be even like Israel, a prince prevailing with God.

Thy Name is my passport, and secures me access;
Thy Name is my plea and secures me answer;
Thy Name is my honor and secures me glory.

Blessed Name, Thou art honey in my mouth, music in my ear, heaven in my heart, and all in all, in all my being.

—Ibid.

CHAPTER SIX

THE WEAPON OF PRAYER

Nothing is more important to God than prayer in dealing with mankind. But it is likewise all-important to man to pray. Failure to pray is failure along the whole line of life. It is failure of duty, service, and spiritual progress. God must help man by prayer. He who does not pray, therefore, robs himself of God's help and places God where He cannot help men. Man must pray to God if love for God is to exist. Faith and hope, and patience and all the strong, beautiful, vital forces of piety are withered and dead in a prayerless life. The life of the individual believer, his personal salvation, and personal Christian graces have their being, bloom and fruitage in prayer.

God's greatest movements in this world have been conditioned on, continued and fashioned by prayer. God has put himself in these great movements just as men have prayed. Present, prevailing, conspicuous and mastering prayer has always brought God to be present. The real and obvious test of a genuine work of God is the prevalence of the spirit of prayer. God's mightiest forces surcharge and impregnate a movement when prayer's mightiest forces are there.

Praying saints are God's agents for carrying on His saving and providential work on earth. If His agents fail Him, neglecting to pray, then His work fails. Praying agents of the Most High are always forerunners of spiritual prosperity.

The men of the Church of all ages who have held the Church for God have had in affluent fullness and richness the ministry of prayer. The rulers of the Church which the Scriptures reveal have had pre-eminence in prayer. Eminent they may have been in culture, in intellect, and in all the natural or human forces; or they may have been lowly in physical attainments and native gifts, yet in each case prayer was the all-potent force in the rulership of the Church. And this was so because God was with and in what they did, for prayer always carries us back to God.

Prayer cannot be retired as a secondary force in this world. To do so is to retire God from the movement. It is to make God secondary. The prayer ministry is an all-engaging force. It must be so, to be a force at all. Prayer is the sense of God's need and the call for God's help to supply that need. The estimate and place of prayer is the estimate and place of God. To give prayer the secondary place is to make God secondary in life's affairs. To substitute other forces for prayer retires God and materializes the whole movement.

Whatever affects the intensity of our praying affects the value of our work. "Too busy to pray" is not only the keynote to backsliding, but it mars even the work done. Nothing is well done without prayer for the simple reason that it leaves God out of the account. It is so easy to be seduced by the good to the neglect of the best, until both the good and the best perish. How easily may men, even leaders in Zion, be led by the insidious wiles of Satan to cut short our praying in the interests of the work! How easy to neglect prayer or abbreviate our praying simply by the plea that we have church work on our hands. Satan has effectively disarmed us when he can keep us too busy doing things to stop and pray.

Apostolic preaching cannot be carried on unless there be apostolic praying. Alas, that this plain truth has been so easily forgotten by those who minister in holy things! How easy to slip away from the closet! Even the apostles had to guard themselves at that point. How much do we need to watch ourselves at that same place! Things legitimate and right may become wrong when they take the place of prayer. Things right in themselves may become wrong things when they are allowed to fasten themselves inordinately upon our hearts. It is not only the sinful things which hurt prayer. It is not alone questionable things which are to be guarded against. But it is things which are right in their places but which are allowed to sidetrack prayer and shut the closet door, often with the self-comforting plea that "we are too busy to pray." The apostles drove directly at this point, and determined that even church business should not affect their praying habits. Prayer must come first. Then would they be in deed and truth God's real agents in this world, through whom He could effectually work, because they were praying men, and thereby put themselves directly in line with His plans and purposes, which were that He works through praying men.

Prayer affects three different spheres of existence— the divine, the angelic and the human. It puts God to work, it puts angels to work, and it puts men to work. It lays its hands upon God, angels and men. What a wonderful reach there is in prayer! It brings into play the forces of heaven and earth. God, angels, and men are subjects of this wonderful law of prayer, and all these have to do with the possibilities and the results of prayer. God has so far placed himself subject to the prayer that by reason of His own appointment, He is induced to work among men in a way in which He does not work if men do not pray. Prayer lays hold upon God and influences Him to work. This is the meaning of prayer as it concerns God. This is the doctrine of prayer, or else there is nothing whatever in prayer.

To no other energy is the promise of God committed as to that of prayer. Upon no other force are the purposes of God so dependent as this one of prayer. The Word of God dilates on the results and necessity of prayer. The work of God stays or advances as prayer puts forth its strength. Prophets and apostles have urged the utility, force and necessity of prayer. "I have set watchmen upon thy walls, O Jerusalem, which shall never hold their peace day nor night: ye that make mention of the Lord, keep not silence, and give him no rest, till he establish, and till he make Jerusalem a praise in the earth."

Prayer puts God's work in His hands, and keeps it there. It looks to Him constantly and depends on Him implicitly to further His own cause. Prayer is but faith resting in, acting with, and leaning on and obeying God. This is why God loves it so well, why He puts all power into its hands, and why He so highly esteems men of prayer. Prayer is a high privilege, a royal prerogative and manifold and eternal are the losses by failure to exercise it.

One of the constitutional enforcements of the gospel is prayer. Without prayer, the gospel can neither be preached effectively, promulgated faithfully, experienced in the heart, nor be practiced in the life. And for the very simple reason that by leaving prayer out of the catalogue of religious duties, we leave God out, and His work cannot progress without Him.

Praying men are essential to Almighty God in all His plans and purposes. God's secrets, councils and cause have never been committed to prayerless men. Neglect of prayer has always brought loss of faith, loss of love, and loss of prayer. Failure to pray has been the baneful, inevitable cause of backsliding and estrangement from God. Prayerless men have stood in the way of God fulfilling His Word and doing His will on earth. They tie the divine hands and interfere with God in His gracious designs. As praying men are a help to God, so prayerless men are a hindrance to Him.

Men are demanded for the great work of soul-saving, and men must go. It is no angelic, impersonal force which is needed. Human hearts baptized with the spirit of prayer, must bear the burden of this message, and human tongues on fire at the result of earnest, persistent prayer, must declare the Word of God to dying men.

The Church today needs praying men to execute her solemn and pressing responsibility to meet the fearful crisis which is facing her. The crying need of the times is for men, in increased numbers—God-fearing men, praying men, Holy Ghost men, men who can endure hardness, who will not count their lives dear unto themselves, but count all things but dross for the excellency of the knowledge of Jesus Christ the Saviour. Praying men are the only men who have influence with God, the only kind of men to whom God commits himself and His gospel. Praying men are the only men in which the Holy Spirit dwells, for the Holy Spirit and prayer go hand-in-hand. The Holy Spirit never descends upon prayerless men. He never fills them; He never empowers them. There is nothing whatever in common between the Spirit of God and men who do not pray. The Spirit dwells only in a prayer atmosphere.

In doing God's work there is no substitute for praying. The men of prayer cannot be displaced with other kinds of men. Men of financial skill, men of education, men of worldly influence—none of these can possibly be put in substitution for the men of prayer. The life, the vigour, the motive power of God's work is formed by praying men. A vitally diseased heart is not a more fearful symptom of approaching death than non-praying men are of spiritual atrophy.

The entire consecration of many of God's children stands out distinctly like towering mountain peaks. Why this? How did they ascend to these heights? What brought them so near to God? What made them so Christlike? The answer is easy—prayer. They prayed much, prayed long, and drank deeper and deeper still. They asked, they sought, and they knocked, till heaven opened its richest inner treasures of grace to them. Prayer was the Jacob's Ladder by which they scaled those holy and blessed heights, and the way by which the angels of God came down to and ministered to them.

They valued praying. It was more precious to them than all jewels, more excellent than any good, more to be valued than the greatest good of earth. They esteemed it, valued it, prized it, *and did it.* They pressed it to its farthest limits, tested its greatest results, and secured its most glorious patrimony. To them prayer was the one thing to be appreciated and used.

Prayer is the genius and mainspring of life. We pray as we live; we live as we pray. Life will never be finer than the quality of the closet. The mercury of life will rise only by the warmth of the closet. Persistent non-praying eventually will depress life below zero. To measure and weigh the conditions of prayer is readily to discover why men do not pray in larger numbers. The conditions are so perfect, so blessed, that it is a rare character who can meet them. A heart all love, a heart that holds even to its enemies in loving contemplation and prayerful concern, a heart from which all bitterness, revenge and envy are purged—how rare! Yet this is the only condition of

mind and heart in which a man can expect to command
the efficacy of prayer. There are certain conditions laid
down for authentic praying. Men are to pray, "lifting
up holy hands," hands here being the symbol of life.
Hands unsoiled by stains of evil doing are the emblem
of a life unsoiled by sin. Thus are men to come into
the presence of God, thus are they to approach the
throne of the Highest, where they can "obtain mercy
and find grace to help in time of need." Here, then,
is one reason why men do not pray. They are too
worldly in heart and too secular in life to enter the
closet; and even though they enter there, they cannot
offer the "effectual, fervent prayer of a righteous
man, [which] availeth much."

Again, "hands" are the symbols of supplication.
Outstretched hands stand for an appeal for help. It is
a silent yet eloquent attitude of the helpless soul
standing before God, appealing for mercy and grace.
"Hands," too, are symbols of activity, power and conduct. Hands outstretched to God in prayer must be
"holy hands," unstained hands. The word "holy" here
means undefiled, unspotted, untainted, and religiously
observing every obligation. How far remote is all this
from the character of the sin-loving, worldly-minded,
fleshly-disposed men soiled by fleshly lusts, spotted
by worldly indulgence, unholy in heart and conduct!
"He who seeks equity must do equity," is the maxim of
earthly courts. So he who seeks God's good gifts must
practice God's good deeds. This is a maxim of heavenly
courts.

Prayer is sensitive and always affected by the character and conduct of him who prays. Water cannot

rise above its own level, and the spotless prayer cannot flow from the spotted heart. Straight praying is never born of crooked conduct. The men, what men are behind their praying, that gives character to their supplication. The craven heart cannot do brave praying. Soiled men cannot make clean, pure supplication.

It is neither words, nor faults, nor ideas, nor feelings, which shape praying, but character and conduct. Men must walk in upright fashion in order to be able to pray well. Bad character and unrighteous living break down praying until it becomes a mere shibboleth. Praying takes its tone and vigour from the life of the man or the woman exercising it. When character and conduct are at a low ebb, praying can but barely live, much less thrive. Prayer must be broad in its scope—it must plead for others. Intercession for others is the hallmark of all true prayer. When prayer is confined to self and to the sphere of one's personal needs, it dies by reason of its littleness, narrowness, and selfishness. Prayer must be broad and unselfish or it will perish. Prayer is the soul of man stirred to plead with God for men. In addition to being interested in the eternal interests of one's own soul it must, in its very nature, be concerned for the spiritual and eternal welfare of others. One's ability to pray for self finds it climaxed in the compassion of its concern expressed for others.

Prayer has a higher origin than man's nature. This is true whether man's nature as separate from the angelic nature, or man's carnal nature unrenewed and unchanged be meant. Prayer does not originate in

the realms of the carnal mind. Such a nature is
entirely foreign to prayer simply because "the carnal
mind is enmity against God." It is by the new spirit
that we pray, the new spirit sweetened by the sugar
of heaven, perfumed with the fragrance of the upper
world, and invigorated by a breath from the Crystal
Sea. The "new spirit" is native to the skies, panting
after heavenly things, inspired by the breath of God.
It is the praying temper from which all the old juices
of the carnal, unregenerate nature have been expelled,
and the fire of God has created the flame which has
consumed worldly lusts, and the juices of the Spirit
have been injected into the soul, and the praying is
entirely divorced from wrath.

The wonderful experience and glory of the Transfiguration was preceded by prayer, and was the result of
the praying of our Lord. What words He used as He
prayed we know not, nor do we know for what He
prayed. But doubtless it was night, and long into
its hours the Master prayed. It was while He prayed
the darkness fled, and His form was lit with unearthly
splendor. Moses and Elijah came to yield to Him
not only the palm of law and prophecy, but the palm
of praying. None other prayed as did Jesus nor had
any such glorious manifestation of the divine presence
or heard so clearly the revealing voice of the Father,
"This is my beloved Son; hear ye him." Happy disciples
to be with Christ in the school of prayer!

How many of us have failed to come to this glorious
mount of transfiguration because we were unacquainted
with the transfiguring power of prayer! It is the going

apart to pray, the long, intense seasons of prayer, in
which we engage which makes the face to shine,
transfigures the character, and makes even dull, earthly
garments to glisten with heavenly splendor. But more
than this: It is real praying which makes eternal
things real, close and tangible, and which brings
the glorified visitors and the heavenly visions. Transfigured lives would not be so rare if there were more
of this transfigured praying. These heavenly visits
would not be so few if there was more of this transfigured praying.

The thing far above all other things in the equipment of the preacher is prayer. Before everything else,
he must be a man who makes a specialty of prayer.
A prayerless preacher is a misnomer. He has either
missed his calling, or has grievously failed God who
called him into the ministry. God wants men who
are not ignoramuses, but those who "study to show
themselves approved." Preaching the Word is essential;
social qualities are not to be underestimated, and education is good; but under and above all else, prayer must
be the main plank in the platform of the man who goes
forth to preach the unsearchable riches of Christ to
a lost and hungry world. The one weak spot in our
church institution lies just here. Prayer is not regarded
as being the primary factor in church life and activity;
and other things, good in their places, are made primary. First things need to be put first, and the first
thing in the equipment of a minister is prayer.

No feeble or secondary place was given to prayer
in the ministry of Jesus. It comes first—emphatic,

conspicuous, controlling. Of prayerful habits, of a prayerful spirit, given to long solitary communion with God, Jesus was above all else, a man of prayer. The crux of His earthly history, in New Testament terminology, is condensed to a single statement, to be found in Hebrews 5:7: "Who in the days of his flesh, when he had offered up prayers and supplications with strong crying and tears, unto him that was able to save him from death, and was heard in that he feared."

He did not ask to be excused from the burden of prayer; He gladly accepted it, acknowledged its claims and voluntarily subjected himself to its demands.

His leadership was pre-eminent, and His praying was pre-eminent. Had it not been, His leadership had been neither pre-eminent nor divine. If, in true leadership, prayer had been dispensable, then certainly Jesus could have dispensed with it. But He did not, nor can. any of His followers who desire effectiveness in Christian activity do other than follow their Lord.

All ability to talk to men is measured by the ability with which a preacher can talk to God for men. He "who plows not in his closet, will never reap in his pulpit." The fact must ever be kept in the forefront and emphasized that Jesus Christ trained His disciples to pray. This is the real meaning of that saying, "the training of the twelve." It must be kept in mind that Christ taught the world's preachers more about praying than He did about preaching. Prayer was the great factor in the spreading of His gospel. Prayer conserved and made efficient all other factors. Yet He did not discount preaching when He stressed praying, but rather talked of the utter dependence of preaching on prayer.

"The Christian's trade is praying," declared Martin Luther. Every Jewish boy had to learn a trade. Jesus Christ learned two: the trade of a carpenter, and that of praying. The one trade subserved earthly uses; the other served His divine and higher purposes. Jewish custom committed Jesus when a boy to the trade of a carpenter; the law of God bound Him to praying from His earliest years, and remained with Him to the end.

The heart is the lexicon of prayer, the life the best commentary on prayer, and the outward bearing its fullest expression. The character is made by prayer; the life is perfected by prayer. And this the ministry needs to learn as thoroughly as the layman. There is but one rule for both.

Blessed is the preacher whose pulpit and closet are hard by each other, and who goes from the one into the other. To consecrate no place to prayer is to make a beggarly showing, not only in praying, but in holy living, for secret prayer and holy living are so closely joined that they can never be dissevered. A preacher or a Christian may live a decent, religious life, without secret prayer, but decency and holiness are two widely different things. And the latter is obtained only by secret prayer.

Prayer should be the inseparable accompaniment of all missionary effort, and must be the one equipment of the missionaries as they go out to their fields of labor, and enter upon their delicate and responsible tasks. Prayer and missions go hand-in-hand. A prayerless missionary is a failure before he goes out, while he is out, and when he returns to his native land. A prayerless board of missions, too, needs to learn the lesson of the necessity of prayer.

The revelations of God to him who is of a prayerful spirit go far beyond the limits of the praying. God commits himself to answer the specific prayer, but He does not stop there. He says, "Ask of me things to come concerning my sons, and concerning the work of my hands, command ye me." Think over that remarkable engagement of God to those who pray. "Command ye me." He actually places himself at the command of praying preachers and a praying Church. And this is a sufficient answer to all doubts, fears, and unbelief, and a wonderful inspiration to do God's work in His own way, which means by the way of prayer.

All of God's called men in the ministry are privileged to stretch their prayers into regions where neither words nor thoughts can go, and are permitted to expect from Him beyond their praying, and for their praying, God himself, and then in addition, "Great and mighty things which thou knowest not."

Real heart-praying, live-praying, praying by the power of the Spirit, direct, specific, ardent, simple praying—this is the kind which legitimately belongs to the pulpit.

There is no school in which to learn to pray in public but in the closet. Preachers who have learned to pray in the closet have mastered the secret of pulpit praying. It is but a short step from the secret praying to effectual, live, pulpit praying. Good pulpit praying follows from good secret praying. A closed closet with the preacher makes for cold, spiritless, formal praying in the pulpit. Study how to pray, oh preacher, but not by studying the forms of prayer, but by attending the school of prayer on your knees before God. Here is where we learn not only to pray before God, but learn also how to pray in the presence of men. He who has learned the way to the closet has discovered the way to pray when he enters the pulpit.

Where are we? What are we doing? Preaching is the very loftiest work possible for a man to do. And praying goes hand-in-hand with preaching. It is a mighty, lofty work. Preaching is a life-giving work, sowing the seeds of eternal life. Oh, may we do it well, do it after God's order, do it successfully!

The gospel of Jesus has neither relish nor life in it when spoken by prayerless lips or handled by prayerless hands. Without prayer the doctrines of Christ degenerate into dead orthodoxy. Preaching them without the aid of the Spirit of God, who comes into the preacher's messages only by prayer, is nothing more than mere lecturing, with no life, no grip, no force in preaching. It amounts to nothing more than live rationalism or sickly sentimentalism. "But we will give ourselves continually to prayer and to the ministry of the word," was the settled and declared purpose of the apostolic ministry. The Kingdom of God waits on prayer, and prayer puts wings on the gospel and power into it. By prayer it moves forward with conquering force and rapid advance.

The Bible preacher prays. He is filled with the Holy Spirit, filled with God's Word, and is filled with faith. He has faith in God, faith in God's only begotten Son, his personal Saviour, and he has implicit faith in God's Word. He cannot do otherwise than pray. He cannot be other than a man of prayer. The breath of his life and the pulsations of his heart are prayer. The Bible preacher lives by prayer, loves by prayer, and preaches by prayer. His bended knees in the place of secert prayer advertise what kind of preacher he is. It is a comparatively easy task for preachers to become so absorbed in the material and external affairs of the church as to lose sight of their own souls, forget the necessity of prayer so needful to keep their own souls alive to God, and lose the inward sweetness of a Christian experience. The prayer which makes much of our preaching must itself be made much of. The character of our praying will determine the character of our preaching. Serious praying will give serious weight to preaching. Prayer makes preaching strong, gives it unction and makes it stick. In every ministry weighty for good, prayer has always been a serious business prophetic of good.

In the school of prayer only can the heart learn to preach. No gifts, no learning, no brain-force, can atone for the failure to pray. No earnestness, no diligence, no study, no amount of social service, will supply its lack. Talking to men for God may be a great thing, and may be very commendable. But talking to God for men is far more valuable and commendable.

The power of Bible preaching lies not simply or solely in superlative devotion to God's Word, and jealous passion for God's truth. All these are essential, valuable, helpful. But above all these things, there must be the sense of the divine presence, and a consciousness of the divine power of God's Spirit on the preacher and in him. He must have an anointing, an empowering, a sealing of the Holy Spirit, for the great work of preaching, making him akin to God's voice, and giving him the energy of God's right hand, so that this Bible preacher can say, "Thy words were found, and I did eat them; and thy word was unto me the joy and rejoicing of my heart. For I am called by thy name, O Lord of hosts."

The "power from on high" may be found in combination with all sources of human power, but is not to be confounded with them, is not dependent upon them, and must never be superseded by them. Whatever of human gift, talent or force a preacher may possess, it is not to be made paramount, or even conspicuous. It must be hidden, lost, overshadowed, by this "power from on high." The forces of intellect and culture may all be present, but without this inward, heaven-given power, all spiritual effort is vain and unsuccessful. Even when lacking the other equipment but having this "power from on high," a preacher cannot but succeed. It is the one essential, all-important vital force which a messenger of God must possess to give wings to his message, to put life into his preaching, and to enable him to speak the Word with acceptance and power.

This "unction of the Holy One" delivers from dryness, saves from superficiality, and gives authority to preaching. It is the one quailty which distinguishes the preacher of the gospel from other men who speak in public; it is that which makes a sermon unique, unlike the deliverance of any other public speaker.

Preachers of the present age excel those of the past in many, possibly in all, human elements of success. They are well-abreast of the age in learning, research, and intellectual vigour. But these things neither insure "power from on high" nor guarantee a live, thriving religious experience or righteous life.

If prayerless men be found in the pew, then it hurts the preacher, robs him of invaluable help, and interferes seriously with the success of his work. How great the need of a praying church to help on the preaching of the Word of the Lord! Both pew and pulpit are jointly concerned in this preaching business. It is a co-partnership. The two go hand-in-hand. One must help the other, one can hinder the other. Both must work in perfect accord or serious damage will result, and God's plan concerning the preacher and the preached Word be defeated.

Men in the pew given to praying for the preacher are like the poles which hold up the wires along which the electric current runs. They are not the power, neither are they the specific agents in making the Word of the Lord effective. But they hold up the wires upon which the divine power runs to the hearts of men. They give liberty to the preacher, exemption from being straightened, and keep him from "getting in the brush." They make conditions favorable for the preaching of the gospel. The Apostle Paul did not desire to fall short of that most important quality in a preacher of the gospel, namely, boldness. He was no coward, or time-server, or man-pleaser, but he needed prayer, in order that he might not, through any kind of timidity, fail to declare the whole truth of God, or through fear of men, declare it in an apologetic, hesitating way. He desired to remove himself as far as possible from an attitude of this kind. His constant desire and effort was to declare the gospel with consecrated boldness and with freedom.

The Possibilities
Of Prayer

If Jacob's desire had been given him in time to get a good night's sleep, he might never have become the prince of pray-ers we know today. If Hannah's prayer for a son had been answered at the time she set for herself, the nation might never have known the mighty man of God it found in Samuel. Hannah wanted only a son, but God wanted more. He wanted a prophet, and a saviour, and a ruler for His people. Someone said that "God had to get a woman before He could get a man." This woman He got in Hannah precisely by delaying the answer to her prayer, for out of the discipline of those weeks and months and years there came a woman with a vision like God's, with tempered soul and gentle spirit and a seasoned will prepared to be the kind of a mother for the kind of a man God knew the nation needed.

—*W. E. Biederwolf*

CHAPTER SEVEN

THE POSSIBILITIES OF PRAYER

The promises of God are "exceeding great and precious," words which clearly indicate their great value and their broad reach, as grounds upon which to base our expectations in praying. Howsoever exceeding great and precious they are, their realization, the possibility and condition of that realization, are based on prayer. How glorious are these promises to the believing saints and to the whole Church! How the brightness and bloom, the fruitage and cloudless midday glory of the future beam on us through the promises of God! Yet these promises never brought hope to bloom or to fruit to a prayerless heart. Neither could these promises. were they thousand-fold increased in number and preciousness, bring millennium glory to a prayerless church. Prayer makes the promise rich, fruitful and a conscious reality.

Prayer as a spiritual energy, and illustrated in its enlarged and mighty working. makes way for and brings into practical realization the promises of God. God's promises cover all things which pertain to life and godliness, which relate to body and soul, which

177

have to do with time and eternity. These promises bless the present and stretch out in their benefactions to the illimitable and eternal future. Prayer holds these promises in keeping and in fruition. Promises are God's golden fruit to be plucked by the hand of prayer. Promises are God's incorruptible seed, to be sown and tilled by prayer.

The promise of God is fulfilled. But it took that all night of importunate praying to do the deed. It took that fearful night of wrestling on Jacob's part to make the promise sure and cause it to bear fruit. Prayer wrought the marvelous deed. So prayer of the same kind will produce like results in this day. It was God's promise and Jacob's praying which crowned and crowded the results so wondrously. Our prayers are too little and feeble to execute the purposes or to claim the promises of God with appropriating power. Marvelous purposes need marvelous praying to execute them. Miracle-making promises need miracle-making prayer to realize them. Only divine praying can operate divine promises or carry out divine purposes.

Let it be noted that prayer gives the promises their efficiency, localizes and appropriates them, and utilizes them. Prayer puts the promises to practical and present uses.

Prayer puts the promises as the seed in the fructifying soil. Promises, like the rain, are general. Prayer embodies, precipitates, and locates them for personal use. Prayer goes by faith into the great fruit orchard of God's exceeding great and precious promises, and with hand and heart picks the ripest and richest fruit. The promises, like electricity, may sparkle and dazzle, yet be impotent for good till these dynamic, life-giving currents are chained by prayer, and are made the mighty forces which move and bless.

In this connection let it be noted that God's promises are always personal and specific. They are not general, indefinite, vague. They do not have to do with multitudes and classes of people in a mass, but are directed to individuals. They deal with persons. Each believer can claim the promise as his own. God deals with each one personally. So every saint can put the promises to the test. "Prove me now herewith, saith the Lord." No need of generalizing, nor of being lost in vagueness. The praying saint has the right to put his hand upon the promise and claim it as his own, one made especially for him, and one intended to embrace all his need, present and future.

How vast are the possibilities of prayer! How wide its reach! What great things are accomplished by this divinely appointed means of grace! It lays its hand on Almighty God and moves Him to do what He would not otherwise do if prayer was not offered. It brings things to pass which would never otherwise occur. The story of prayer is the story of great achievement. Prayer is a wonderful power placed by Almighty God in the hands of His saints, which may be used to accomplish great purposes and to achieve unusual results. Prayer reaches to everything, takes in all things great and small which are promised by God to the children of men. The only limits to prayer are the promises of God and His ability to fulfill those promises. "Open thy mouth wide and I will fill it."

The records of prayer's achievements are encouraging to faith, cheering to the expectations of saints, and are an inspiration to all who would pray and test its values. Prayer is no mere untried theory. It is not some strange unique scheme, concocted in the brains of men, and set on foot by them, an invention which has never been tried nor put to the test.

Prayer is a divine arrangement in the moral government of God, designed for the benefit of men and intended as a means for furthering the interests of His Cause on earth, and carrying out His gracious purposes in redemption and providence.

Prayer proves itself. It is susceptible of proving its virtues by those who pray.

Prayer needs no proof other than its accomplishments. "If any man will do his will, he shall know of the doctrine." If any man will know the virtue of prayer, if he will know what it will do, let him pray. Let him put prayer to the test.

What a breadth is given to prayer! What heights it reaches! It is the breathing of a soul inflamed for God, and inflamed for men. It goes as far as the gospel goes, and is as wide, compassionate and prayerful as is that gospel.

How much of prayer do all these unpossessed, alienated provinces of earth demand in order to enlighten them, to impress them and to move them toward God and His Son, Jesus Christ? Had the professed disciples of Christ only prayed in the past as they ought to have done, the centuries would not have found the provinces still bound in death, in sin, and in ignorance.

Alas! How the unbelief of men has limited the power of God to work through prayer! What limitations have disciples of Jesus Christ put upon prayer by their prayerlessness! How the Church, with her neglect of prayer, has hedged about the gospel and shut up doors of access!

Prayer possibilities open doors for the entrance of the gospel: "With all praying also for us that God would open to us a door of utterance." Prayer opened for the apostles doors of utterance, created opportunities and made openings to preach the gospel. The appeal by prayer was to God, because God was moved by prayer. God was thereby moved to do His own work in an enlarged way and by new ways. Prayer possibility gives not only great power, and opens doors to the gospel, but it gives facility as well to the gospel.

Prayer makes the gospel to go fast and to move with glorious fastness. A gospel projected by the mighty energies of prayer is neither slow, lazy nor dull. It moves with God's power, with God's effulgence and with angelic swiftness.

The possibilities of prayer reach to all things. Whatever concerns man's highest welfare, and whatever has to do with God's plans and purposes concerning men on earth, is a subject for prayer. In "whatsoever ye shall ask," is embraced all that concerns us or the children of men and God. And whatever is left out of "whatsoever" is left out of prayer. Where will we draw the lines which leave out all which will limit the word "whatsoever"? Define it and search out and publish the things which the Word does not include. If "whatsoever" does not include all things, then add to it the word "anything." "If ye shall ask anything in my name, I will do it."

The benefits, the possibilities and the necessity of prayer are not merely subjective but are peculiarly objective in their characters.

Prayer aims at a definite object. Prayer has a direct design in view. Prayer always has something specific before the mind's eye. There may be some subjective benefits which acrue from praying, but this is altogether secondary and incidental. Prayer always drives directly at an object and seeks to secure a desired end.

Prayer is asking, seeking and knocking at a door for something we have not, which we desire, and which God has promised to us.

Prayer is a direct address to God. "In everything let your requests be made known unto God."

Prayer secures blessings, and makes men better because it reaches the ear of God.

Prayer is only for the betterment of men when it has affected God and moved Him to do something for men. Prayer affects men by affecting God. Prayer moves men because it moves God to move men. Prayer influences men by influencing God to influence them.

Prayer moves the hand that moves the world.

The possibilities of prayer are the possibilities of faith. Prayer and faith are Siamese twins. One heart animates them both. Faith is always praying. Prayer is always believing.

Faith must have a tongue by which it can speak. Prayer is the tongue of faith. Faith must receive. Prayer is the hand of faith stretched out to receive. Prayer must rise and soar. Faith must give prayer the wings to fly and soar.

Prayer must have an audience with God. Faith opens the door, and access and audience are given.

Prayer asks. Faith lays its hands on the thing asked for. Prayer is not an indifferent or a small thing. It is not a sweet little privilege. It is a great prerogative, far-reaching in its effects. Failure to pray entails losses far beyond the person who neglects it.

Prayer is not a mere episode of the Christian life. Rather the whole life is a preparation for and the result of prayer. In its condition, prayer is the sum of religion. Faith is but a channel of prayer. Faith gives it wings and swiftness.

Prayer is the lungs through which holiness breathes.

Prayer is not only the language of spiritual life, but makes its very essence and forms its real character.

"Oh for a faith that will not shrink
Though pressed by every foe;
That will not tremble on the brink
Of any earthly woe.

"Lord, give me such a faith as this,
And then, whate'er may come,
I'll taste e'en here, the hallowed bliss
Of my eternal home."

He who has the spirit of prayer has the highest interest in the court of heaven. And the only way to retain it is to keep it in constant employment. *Apostasy begins in the closet.* No man ever backslid from the life and power of Christianity who continued constant and fervent in private prayer. He "who prays without ceasing is likely to rejoice evermore."—Adam Clark

For all these evils, prayer is the one universal remedy. Pure praying remedies all ills, cures all diseases, relieves all situations, however dire, most calamitous, most fearful and despairing. Prayer to God, pure praying, relieves dire situations because God can relieve when no one else can. Nothing is too hard for God. No cause is hopeless which God undertakes. No case is mortal when Almighty God is the physician. No conditions are despairing which can deter or defy God.

Jacob is an illustration for all time of the commanding and conquering forces of prayer. God came to him as an antagonist. He grappled Jacob and shook him as if he were in the embrace of a deadly foe. Jacob, the deceitful supplanter, the wily, unscrupulous trader, had no eyes to see God. His perverted principles, and his deliberate over-reaching and wrong-doing had blinded his vision.

To reach God, to know God, and to conquer God, that was the demand of this critical hour. Jacob was alone, and all night witnessed to the intensity of the struggle, its changing issues, and its veering fortunes, as well as the receding and advancing lines in the conflict. Here was the strength and weakness, the power of self-despair, the energy of perseverance, the elevation of humility, and the victory of surrender. Jacob's salvation issued from the forces which he massed in that all-night conflict.

He prayed and wept and importuned until the fiery hate of Esau's heart died and it was softened into love. A greater miracle was wrought on Jacob than on Esau. His name, his character and his destiny were all changed by that all-night praying. Here is the record of the results of that night's praying struggle: "As a prince hast thou power with God and with men, and hast prevailed." "By his strength he had power with God, yea, he had power over the angel and prevailed."

What forces lie in importunate prayer! What mighty results are gained by it in one night's struggle in praying! God is affected and changed in attitude and two men are transformed in character and destiny.

"Satan dreads nothing but prayer—The church that lost its Christ was full of good works. Activities are multiplied that meditation may be ousted, and organizations are increased that prayer may have no chance. Souls may be lost in good works, as surely as in evil ways. *The one concern of the devil is to keep the saints from prayer.* He fears nothing from prayerless studies, prayerless work, prayerless religion. He laughs at our toil, mocks at our wisdom, *but trembles when we pray.*"—Samuel Chadwick

The promise reads, and we cannot too often refer to it, for it is the very basis of our faith and the ground on which we stand when we pray: "All things whatsoever ye ask in prayer, believing, ye shall receive." What enumeration table can tabulate, itemize, and aggregate "All things whatsoever"? The possibilities of prayer and faith go to the length of the endless chain, and cover the unmeasurable area.

Prayer in its legitimate possibilities goes out on God himself. Prayer goes out with faith not only in the promise of God, but faith in God himself, and in God's ability to do. Prayer goes out not on the promise merely, but "obtains promises," and creates promises. If Christians prayed as Christians ought, with strong commanding faith, with earnestness and sincerity, men, God-called men, God-empowered men everywhere, would be all burning to go and spread the gospel world-wide. The Word of the Lord would run and be glorified as never known heretofore. The God-influenced men, the God-inspired men, the God-commissioned men, would go and kindle the flame of sacred fire for Christ, salvation and heaven, everywhere in

all nations, and soon all men would hear the glad
tidings of salvation and have an opportunity to receive
Jesus Christ as their personal Saviour. Let us read
another one of those large, illimitable statements in
God's Word, which is a direct challenge to prayer and
faith: "He that spared not his own Son, but delivered
him up for us all, how shall he not with him also freely
give us all things?"

What a basis have we here for prayer and faith,
illimitable, measureless in breadth, in depth and in
height! The promise to give us all things is backed
up by the calling to our remembrance of the fact
that God freely gave His only begotten Son for our
redemption. His giving His Son is the assurance and
guarantee that He will freely give all things to him
who believes and prays.

The possibilities of prayer are established by the
fact and the history of prayer. Facts are stubborn
things. Facts are the true things. Theories may be but
speculations. Opinions may be wholly at fault. But
facts must be deferred to. They cannot be ignored.
What are the possibilities of prayer judged by the
facts? What is the history of prayer? What does it
reveal to us? Prayer has a history, written in God's
Word and recorded in the experiences and lives of
God's saints. History is truly teaching by example.
We may miss the truth by perverting the history,
but the truth is in the facts of history. God reveals
the truth by the facts. God reveals himself by the facts
of religious history. God teaches us His will by the
facts and examples of Bible history. God's facts, God's
Word, and God's history are all in perfect harmony,

and have much of God in them all. God has ruled
the world by prayer; and God still rules the world
by the same divinely ordained means.

Paul gives the various terms of prayer, supplication
and giving of thanks as the complement of true praying. The soul must be in all of these spiritual exercises.
There must be no half-hearted praying, no abridging
its nature, and no abating its force, if we would be
freed from this undue anxiety which causes friction
and internal distress, and if we would receive the
rich fruit of that peace which passeth all understanding.
He who prays must be an earnest soul, all round in
spiritual attributes.

Prayer blesses all things, brings all things, believes
all things and prevents all things. Everything as well
as every place and every hour is to be ordered by
prayer. Prayer has in it the possibility to affect everything which affects us. Here are the vast possibilities
of prayer. How much is the bitter of life sweetened
by prayer! How are the feeble made strong by prayer!
Sickness flees before the health of prayer. Doubts,
misgivings, and trembling fears retire before prayer.
Wisdom, knowledge, holiness and heaven are at the
command of prayer. Nothing is outside of prayer.
It has the power to gain all things in the provision
of our Lord Jesus Christ. Paul covers all departments
and sweeps the entire field of human concernment,
conditions, and happenings by saying, "In everything
by prayer."

The general statement, "The effectual, fervent
prayer of a righteous man availeth much," is a state-

ment of prayer as an energetic force. Two words
are used. One signifies power in exercise, operative
power, while the other is a power as an endowment.
Prayer is power and strength, a power and strength
which influences God, and is most salutary, widespread
and marvelous in its gracious benefits to man. Prayer
influences God. The ability of God to do for man is
the measure of the possibility of prayer.

> "Thou art coming to a King,
> Large petitions with thee bring;
> For His grace and power are such
> None can ever ask too much."

It is answered prayer which brings praying out
of the realm of dry, dead things, and makes praying
a thing of life and power. It is the answer to prayer
which brings things to pass, and changes the natural
trend of things, and orders all things according to the
will of God. It is the answer to prayer which takes
praying out of the regions of fanaticism, and saves
it from being utopian, or from being merely fanciful.
It is the answer to prayer which makes praying a
power for God and for man, and makes praying real
and divine. Unanswered prayers are training schools
for unbelief, an imposition and a nuisance, an im-
pertinence to God and to man.

Answers to prayer are the only surety that we
have prayed aright. What marvelous power there is
in prayer! What untold miracles it works in this
world! What untold benefits to men does it secure to
those who pray! Why is it that the average prayer
by the million goes abegging for an answer?

The answer to prayer is the part of prayer which glorifies God. Unanswered prayers are dumb oracles which leave the praying ones in darkness, doubt and bewilderment, and which carry no conviction to the unbeliever. It is not the act nor the attitude of praying which gives efficacy to prayer. It is not abject prostration of the body before God, the vehement or quiet utterance to God, the exquisite beauty and poetry of the diction of our prayers, which do the deed. It is not the marvelous way of argument and eloquence in praying which makes prayer effectual. Not one or all of these are the things which glorify God. It is the answer which brings glory to His name.

We are rich and strong, good and holy, beneficent and benignant, by answered prayer. It is not the mere performance, the attitude, nor the words of prayer which bring benefit to us, but it is the answer sent directly from heaven. Conscious and real answers to prayer bring real good to us. This is not praying merely for self or simply for selfish ends. The selfish character cannot exist when the prayer conditions are fulfilled.

The wonders of God's power are to be kept alive, made real and present, and repeated only by prayer. God is not now so evident in the world, so almighty in manifestation as of old, not because miracles have passed away, not because God has ceased to work, but because prayer has been shorn of its simplicity, its majesty, and its power. God still lives, and miracles still live while God lives and acts, for miracles are God's way of acting. Prayer is dwarfed, withered, and petrified when faith in God is staggered by doubts of His ability, or through the shrinking caused by fear.

When faith has a telescope, a far-off vision of God, prayer works no miracles, and brings no marvels of deliverance. But when God is seen by faith's closest, fullest eye, prayer makes a history of wonders.

Take another fact showing the wonders of prayer wrought by Almighty God in answer to the praying of His true prophet. A nation of God's people was fearfully apostate in head and heart and life. A man of God went to the apostate king with the fearful message which meant so much to the land, "There shall not be rain nor dew these years but according to my word." Whence this mighty force which can stay the clouds, seal up the rain, and hold back the dew? Who is this who speaks with such authority? Is there any force which can do this on earth? Only one, and that force is prayer, wielded in the hands of a praying prophet of God. It is he who has influence with God and over God in prayer, who thus dares to assume such authority over the forces of nature. This man Elijah is skilled in the use of that tremendous force. "And Elijah prayed earnestly, and it rained not on the earth for three years and six months."

God is everywhere, watching, superintending, overseeing, governing everything in the highest interest of man, and carrying forward His plans and executing His purposes in creation and redemption. He is not an absentee God.

> "Pour out your souls to God,
> And bow them with your knees,
> And spread your hearts and hands abroad
> And pray for Zion's peace;

Your guides and brethren bear
For ever on your mind;
Extend the arms of mighty prayer,
In grasping all mankind."

—Charles Wesley